BEST OF
AMERICA

THE AMERICAN FAMILY COOKING LIBRARY

BEST OF AMERICA

CARLA CAPALBO & LAURA WASHBURN

Photography by AMANDA HEYWOOD

Anness
Publishing

For Marie, my grandmother,
who has always been my inspiration. Carla

ISBN 0-8317-1758-0

Editorial Director: Joanna Lorenz
Project Editor: Carole Clements
Copy Editor: Norma MacMillan
Designer: Sheila Volpe
Photographer: Amanda Heywood
Food Styling: Elizabeth Wolf Cohen,
steps by Marilyn Forbes and Cara Hobday

Printed and bound in China

The publisher wishes to thank Cuisinarts Corporation,
1 Cummings Point Road, Stamford, Connecticut 06904.

CONTENTS

~

INTRODUCTION	6
NEW ENGLAND & MID-ATLANTIC STATES	8
THE SOUTH	48
THE MIDWEST	88
THE SOUTHWEST	128
CALIFORNIA	170
THE NORTHWEST & MOUNTAIN STATES	212
INDEX	252

INTRODUCTION

~

American families – with their diverse culinary traditions – have always been on the move. Hardy immigrants crossed oceans, and pioneers followed a trail or a river to the West. Today we chase down jobs far from where we grew up and retire to where the sun shines. As people criss-cross the country, they adapt their favorite recipes to the local produce and, in mixed communities, adopt entirely new foods and flavors. What has evolved is the richest and most varied cuisine imaginable. Even now, new dishes are continually entering the changing repertoire.

BEST OF AMERICA explores this gastronomic heritage. We take you through America's regional cooking, passing on historical tastes with vintage recipes as well as offering new dishes made with local ingredients. All the recipes are presented in a simple step-by-step format with pictures to guide you every inch of the way.

We have taken the compass points as general divisions and look at each region in terms of its most important and characteristic ingredients and its unique traditions, offering a varied and representative selection of the food from each area.

Cooking from New England and the Mid-Atlantic seaboard evokes some of our oldest food traditions, from the first Thanksgiving to Thomas Jefferson's waffle iron. With such a long coastline, seafood has always played a key role, and cold winters promoted the hearty fare we associate with this region. For many people, the South conjures up Spanish moss, French quarter architecture, and plantations. In fact, the Spanish, French, and African-American influences are the most important ones in terms of local food, and Cajun, Creole, and soul food mingle with customs of gracious dining carried over from earlier times.

Moving westward, the Midwest has always been the breadbasket of the country and, although much fertile farmland has been urbanized today, raising crops and animals for the table is still important. The Southwest draws on heirloom traditions, gleaned from Native Americans and Spanish settlers of the areas. Since the state of California occupies much of the West coast and has had such an influence on culinary trends, we have treated it on its own. With well stocked coastal waters and orchards laden with apples, the Pacific Northwest and the Mountain States conclude the culinary tour.

Today cooking at home has changed from an everyday event starting from scratch to more of a hobby. But whether you're preparing for a festive meal to share with friends or simply putting together a quick dinner, BEST OF AMERICA has recipes to suit.

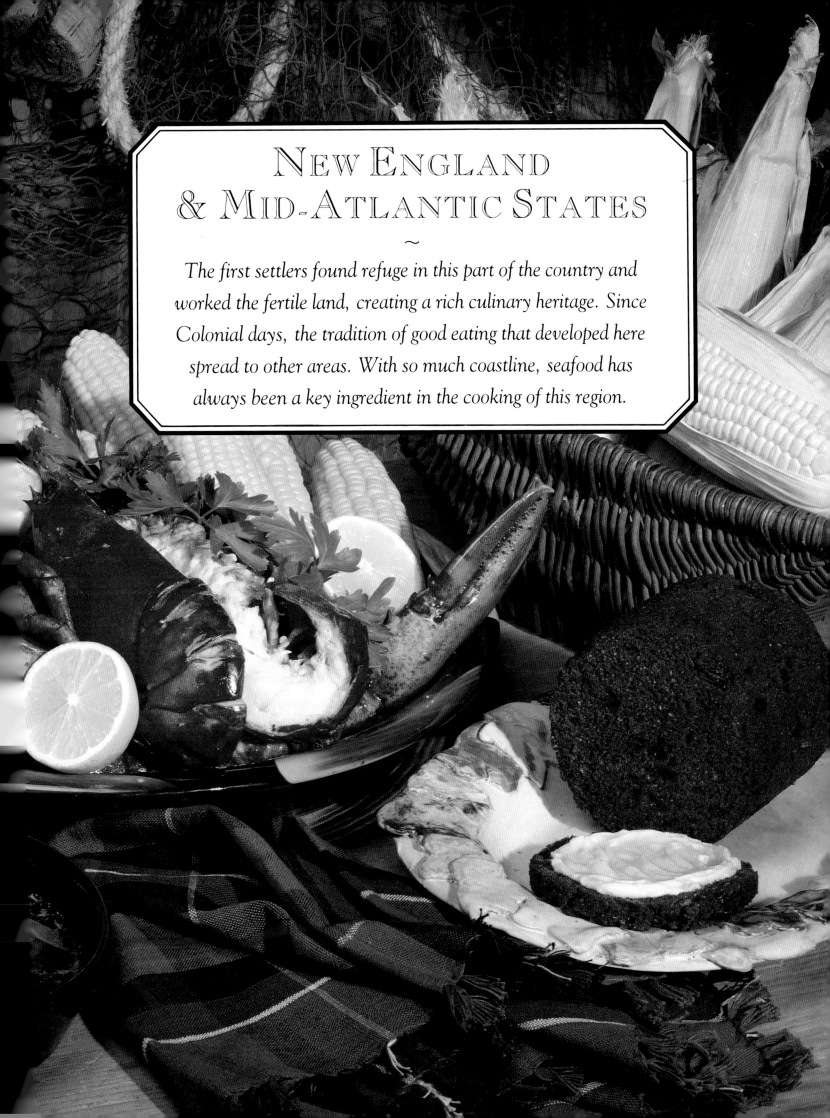

New England & Mid-Atlantic States

~

The first settlers found refuge in this part of the country and worked the fertile land, creating a rich culinary heritage. Since Colonial days, the tradition of good eating that developed here spread to other areas. With so much coastline, seafood has always been a key ingredient in the cooking of this region.

New England Clam Chowder

SERVES 8

4 dozen cherrystone or littleneck clams, scrubbed

6 cups water

¼ cup finely diced salt pork or bacon

1½ cups minced onions

1 bay leaf

2½ cups diced peeled potatoes

salt and pepper

2 cups milk, warmed

1 cup light cream

chopped fresh parsley, for garnishing

1 Rinse the clams well in cold water. Drain. Place them in a deep kettle with the 6 cups of water and bring to a boil. Cover and steam until the shells open, about 10 minutes. Remove from the heat.

2 When the clams have cooled slightly, remove them from their shells. Discard any clams that have not opened. Chop the clams coarsely. Strain the cooking liquid through a strainer lined with cheesecloth, and reserve it.

3 In a large heavy saucepan, fry the salt pork or bacon until it renders its fat and begins to brown. Add the onions and cook over low heat until softened, 8–10 minutes.

4 ▲ Add the bay leaf, potatoes, and clam cooking liquid. Stir. Bring to a boil and cook 5–10 minutes.

5 ▲ Stir in the chopped clams. Continue to cook until the potatoes are tender, stirring occasionally. Season with salt and pepper.

6 Reduce the heat to low and stir in the warmed milk and cream. Simmer very gently 5 minutes more. Discard the bay leaf, and taste and adjust the seasoning before serving, sprinkled with parsley.

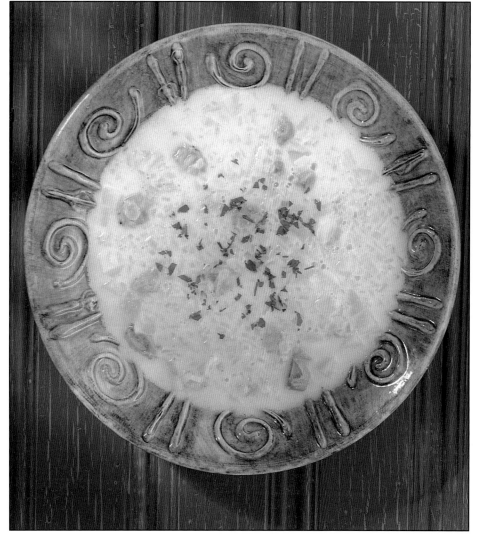

~ COOK'S TIP ~

If clams have been dug, purging helps to rid them of sand and stomach contents. Put them in a bowl of cold water, sprinkle with ½ cup cornmeal and some salt. Stir lightly and let stand in a cool place for 3–4 hours.

Chilled Asparagus Soup

SERVES 6

| 2 pounds fresh asparagus |
| 4 tablespoons butter or olive oil |
| 1½ cups sliced leeks or scallions |
| 3 tablespoons flour |
| 6 cups chicken stock or water |
| salt and pepper |
| ½ cup light cream or plain yogurt |
| 1 tablespoon minced fresh tarragon or chervil |

1 ▲ Cut the top 2½ inches off the asparagus spears. Blanch these tips in boiling water until just tender, 5–6 minutes. Drain. Cut each tip into 2 or 3 pieces, and set aside.

2 Trim the ends of the stalks, removing any brown or woody parts. Chop the stalks into ½-inch pieces.

3 ▲ Heat the butter or oil in a heavy saucepan. Add the leeks or scallions and cook over low heat until softened, 5–8 minutes. Stir in the chopped asparagus stalks, cover, and cook 6–8 minutes more.

4 Add the flour and stir well to blend. Cook 3–4 minutes, uncovered, stirring occasionally.

5 ▼ Add the stock or water. Bring to a boil, stirring frequently, then reduce the heat and simmer 30 minutes. Season with salt and pepper.

6 ▲ Purée the soup in a food processor or food mill. If necessary, strain it to remove any coarse fibers. Stir in the asparagus tips, most of the cream or yogurt, and the herbs. Chill well. Stir thoroughly before serving, and check the seasoning. Garnish with swirled cream or yogurt.

Chesapeake Melon and Crab Meat Salad

SERVES 6

1 pound fresh lump crab meat

½ cup mayonnaise

¼ cup sour cream or plain yogurt

2 tablespoons olive oil

2 tablespoons fresh lemon or lime juice

¼ cup minced scallions

2 tablespoons minced fresh coriander (cilantro)

¼ teaspoon cayenne

salt and pepper

1½ canteloupe or small honeydew melons

3 medium-size heads of Belgian endive

fresh coriander (cilantro) sprigs, for garnishing

1 ▲ Pick over the crab meat very carefully, removing any bits of shell or cartilage. Leave the pieces of crab meat as large as possible.

2 ▲ In a medium-size bowl, combine all the other ingredients except the melon and endive. Mix well. Fold the crab meat into this dressing.

3 ▲ Halve the melons and remove the seeds. Cut into thin slices, and remove the rind.

4 ▲ Arrange the salad on individual serving plates, making a decorative design with the melon slices and whole endive leaves. Place a mound of dressed crab meat on each plate. Garnish each salad with fresh coriander sprigs.

Long Island Scallop and Mussel Kabobs

SERVES 4

5 tablespoons butter, at room temperature

2 tablespoons minced fresh fennel fronds or parsley

1 tablespoon fresh lemon juice

salt and pepper

32 bay or small sea scallops

24 large mussels in shell

8 bacon slices

1 cup fresh bread crumbs

¼ cup olive oil

hot toast, for serving

1 ▲ Make the flavored butter by combining the butter with the minced herbs, lemon juice, and salt and pepper to taste. Mix well. Set aside.

2 ▲ In a small saucepan, cook the scallops in their own liquor until they begin to shrink. (If there is no scallop liquor – retained from the shells after shucking – use a little fish stock or white wine.) Drain and pat dry with paper towels.

3 Scrub the mussels well, and rinse under cold running water. Place in a large saucepan with about 1 inch of water in the bottom. Cover and steam the mussels over medium heat until they open. Remove them from their shells, and pat dry on paper towels. Discard any mussels that have not opened.

4 ▼ Take 8 6-inch wooden or metal skewers. Thread on each one, alternately, 4 scallops, 3 mussels, and a slice of bacon, weaving the bacon between the scallops and mussels.

5 Preheat the broiler.

6 ▲ Spread the bread crumbs on a plate. Brush the seafood with olive oil and roll in the crumbs to coat all over.

7 Place the skewers on the broiler rack. Broil until crisp and lightly browned, 4–5 minutes on each side. Serve immediately with hot toast and the flavored butter.

Oyster Stew

SERVES 6

2 cups milk

2 cups light cream

1 quart shucked oysters, drained, with
    their liquor reserved

⅛ teaspoon paprika

salt and pepper

2 tablespoons butter

1 tablespoon minced fresh parsley

1 Combine the milk, cream, and
oyster liquor in a heavy saucepan.

2 ▼ Heat the mixture over medium
heat until small bubbles appear around
the edge of the pan. Do not allow it to
boil. Reduce the heat to low and add
the oysters.

3 Cook, stirring occasionally, until
the oysters plump up and their edges
begin to curl. Add the paprika, and
salt and pepper to taste.

4 Meanwhile, warm 6 soup plates or
bowls. Cut the butter into 6 pieces
and put one piece in each bowl.

5 Ladle in the oyster stew and
sprinkle with parsley. Serve
immediately, with soda crackers if
desired.

Oysters Rockefeller

SERVES 6

1 pound fresh spinach leaves

½ cup chopped scallions

½ cup chopped celery

½ cup chopped fresh parsley

1 garlic clove

2 anchovy fillets

4 tablespoons butter or margarine

½ cup dry bread crumbs

1 teaspoon Worcestershire sauce

2 tablespoons anise-flavored liqueur
    (Pernod or Ricard)

½ teaspoon salt

hot pepper sauce

36 oysters in shell

fine strips of lemon rind, for garnishing

~ COOK'S TIP ~

To open an oyster push the point
of an oyster knife about ½ inch
into the "hinge". Push down
firmly. The lid should pop open.

---

1 ▲ Wash the spinach well. Drain,
and place in a heavy saucepan. Cover
and cook over low heat until just
wilted. Remove from the heat. When
the spinach is cool enough to handle,
squeeze it to remove excess water.

2 ▲ Put the spinach, scallions,
celery, parsley, garlic, and anchovy
fillets in a food processor and process
until finely chopped.

3 Heat the butter or margarine in a
skillet. Add the spinach mixture,
bread crumbs, Worcestershire sauce,
liqueur, salt, and hot pepper sauce to
taste. Cook 1–2 minutes. Let cool,
and refrigerate until ready to use.

4 Preheat the oven to 450°F. Line a
baking sheet with crumpled foil.

5 ▲ Open the oysters and remove
the top shells. Arrange them, side by
side, on the foil (it will keep them
upright). Spoon the spinach mixture
over the oysters, smoothing the tops
with the back of the spoon.

6 Bake until piping hot, about 20
minutes. Serve immediately,
garnished with lemon rind.

Oyster Stew (top), Oysters Rockefeller

Cape Cod Fried Clams

SERVES 4

36 cherrystone clams, scrubbed

1 cup buttermilk

¼ teaspoon celery salt

¼ teaspoon cayenne

oil for deep-frying

1 cup dry bread crumbs

2 eggs, beaten with 2 tablespoons water

lemon wedges and tartar sauce or
    catsup, for serving

1 Rinse the clams well. Put them in a large kettle with 2 cups of water and bring to a boil. Cover and steam until the shells open.

2 ▼ Remove the clams from their shells, and cut away the black skins from the necks. Discard any clams that have not opened. Strain the cooking liquid and reserve.

3 ▲ Place the buttermilk in a large bowl and stir in the celery salt and cayenne. Add the clams and ½ cup of their cooking liquid. Mix well. Let stand 1 hour.

4 Heat oil in a deep-fryer or large saucepan to 375°F. (To test the temperature without a thermometer, drop in a cube of bread; it should be golden brown in 40 seconds.)

5 ▲ Drain the clams and roll them in the bread crumbs to coat all over. Dip them in the beaten egg and then in the bread crumbs again.

6 Fry the clams in the hot oil, a few at a time, stirring, until they are crisp and brown, about 2 minutes per batch. Remove with a slotted spoon and drain on paper towels.

7 Serve the fried clams hot, accompanied by lemon wedges and tartar sauce or catsup.

Eggs Benedict

SERVES 4

1 teaspoon vinegar

4 eggs

2 English muffins or 4 rounds of bread

butter, for spreading

2 slices of cooked ham, ¼-inch thick,
   each cut in half crosswise

fresh chives, for garnishing

FOR THE SAUCE

3 egg yolks

2 tablespoons fresh lemon juice

¼ teaspoon salt

½ cup (1 stick) butter

2 tablespoons light cream

pepper

4 ▼ Bring a shallow pan of water to a boil. Stir in the vinegar. Break each egg into a cup, then slide it carefully into the water. Delicately turn the white around the yolk with a slotted spoon. Cook until the egg is set to your taste, 3–4 minutes. Remove to paper towels to drain. Very gently cut any ragged edges off the eggs with a small knife or scissors.

5 ▲ While the eggs are poaching, split and toast the muffins or toast the bread slices. Butter while still warm.

6 Place a piece of ham, which you may brown in butter if you wish, on each muffin half or slice of toast. Trim the ham to fit neatly. Place an egg on each ham-topped muffin. Spoon the warm sauce over the eggs, garnish with chives, and serve.

1 ▲ For the sauce, put the egg yolks, lemon juice, and salt in the container of a food processor or blender. Blend 15 seconds.

2 Melt the butter in a small saucepan until it bubbles (do not let it brown). With the motor running, pour the hot butter into the food processor or blender through the feed tube in a slow, steady stream. Turn off the machine as soon as all the butter has been added.

3 Scrape the sauce into the top of a double boiler, over just simmering water. Stir until thickened, 2–3 minutes. (If the sauce curdles, whisk in 1 tablespoon of boiling water.) Stir in the cream and season with pepper. Keep warm over the hot water.

Maryland Crab Cakes with Tartar Sauce

SERVES 4

1½ pounds fresh lump crab meat

1 egg, beaten

2 tablespoons mayonnaise

1 tablespoon Worcestershire sauce

1 tablespoon sherry wine

2 tablespoons minced fresh parsley

1 tablespoon minced fresh chives or dill

salt and pepper

3 tablespoons olive oil

FOR THE SAUCE

1 egg yolk

1 tablespoon white wine vinegar

2 tablespoons Dijon-style mustard

1 cup vegetable or peanut oil

2 tablespoons fresh lemon juice

¼ cup minced scallions

2 tablespoons chopped drained capers

¼ cup minced sour dill pickles

¼ cup minced fresh parsley

1 ▲ Pick over the crab meat, removing any shell or cartilage. Keep the pieces of crab as large as possible.

~ COOK'S TIP ~

For easier handling and to make the crab meat go further, add 1 cup fresh bread crumbs and 1 more egg to the crab mixture. Divide the mixture into 12 cakes to serve 6.

---

2 ▲ In a mixing bowl, combine the beaten egg with the mayonnaise, Worcestershire sauce, sherry, and herbs. Season with salt and pepper. Gently fold in the crab meat.

3 ▲ Divide the mixture into 8 portions and gently form each one into an oval cake. Place on a baking sheet between layers of wax paper and refrigerate at least 1 hour.

4 ▲ Meanwhile, make the sauce. In a medium-size bowl, beat the egg yolk with a wire whisk until smooth. Add the vinegar, mustard, and salt and pepper to taste, and whisk about 10 seconds to blend. Whisk in the oil in a slow, steady stream.

5 ▲ Add the lemon juice, scallions, capers, pickles, and parsley and mix well. Check the seasoning. Cover and chill.

6 Preheat the broiler.

7 ▲ Brush the crab cakes with the olive oil. Place on an oiled baking sheet, in one layer.

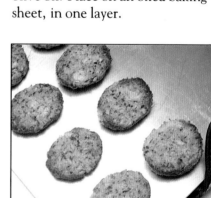

8 ▲ Broil 6 inches from the heat until golden brown, about 5 minutes on each side. Serve the crab cakes hot with the tartar sauce.

Baked Scrod

SERVES 6

2½ pounds scrod or bluefish fillets, skinned

3 tablespoons olive oil

1 teaspoon drained capers

2 garlic cloves

2 medium-size ripe tomatoes, peeled, seeded, and finely diced

2 tablespoons minced fresh basil, or 2 teaspoons dried basil

salt and pepper

1 cup dry white wine

1 Preheat the oven to 400°F.

2 ▲ Arrange the fillets in one layer in a shallow oiled baking dish. Brush the fish with olive oil.

3 Chop the capers with the garlic. Mix with the tomatoes and basil. Season with salt and pepper.

4 ▼ Spoon the tomato mixture over the fish. Pour in the wine. Bake until the fish is cooked, 15–20 minutes. Test for doneness with the point of a knife; the fish should be just opaque in the center. Serve hot.

Old Westbury Flounder with Crab

SERVES 6

4 tablespoons butter or margarine

¼ cup flour

1 cup fish stock, or ¾ cup fish stock mixed with ¼ cup dry white wine

1 cup milk

1 bay leaf

salt and pepper

12 flounder fillets, about 2½ pounds

1½ cups fresh crab meat, flaked

½ cup freshly grated Parmesan cheese

1 Preheat the oven to 425°F.

~ **VARIATIONS** ~

Other flat white fish, such as sole, can be substituted for the flounder. Raw peeled and deveined shrimp, chopped if large, can be used instead of crab meat.

2 ▲ In a medium-size heavy saucepan, melt the butter or margarine over medium heat. Stir in the flour and cook 2–3 minutes.

3 ▲ Pour in the fish stock (or mixed fish stock and wine) and the milk. Whisk until smooth.

4 Add the bay leaf. Raise the heat to medium-high and bring to a boil. Cook 3–4 minutes more. Remove the sauce from the heat, and add salt to taste. Keep hot.

5 ▲ Butter a large baking dish. Twist each fillet to form a "cone" shape and arrange in the dish. Sprinkle the crab meat over the fish. Pour the hot sauce evenly over the top and sprinkle with the cheese.

6 Bake until the top is golden brown and the fish is cooked, 10–12 minutes. Test for doneness with the point of a knife: the fish should be just opaque in the center. Serve hot.

Baked Scrod (top), Old Westbury Flounder with Crab

Scallops Thermidor

SERVES 6

2 pounds sea scallops

½ cup flour

½ cup (1 stick) butter or margarine

1 cup quartered small mushrooms

½ cup fresh bread crumbs

2 tablespoons minced fresh parsley

2 tablespoons minced fresh chives

½ cup sherry wine

¼ cup cognac

1 teaspoon Worcestershire sauce

½ teaspoon salt

¼ teaspoon black pepper

1½ cups whipping cream

2 egg yolks

chives, for garnishing

1 Preheat the oven to 400°F.

2 ▲ Roll the scallops in the flour, shaking off the excess. Heat half of the butter or margarine in a medium-size skillet. Add the scallops and sauté until they are barely golden all over, about 3 minutes. Remove from the skillet and set aside.

3 ▲ Melt 2 more tablespoons of butter or margarine in the pan. Add the mushrooms and bread crumbs and sauté 3–4 minutes, stirring. Add the parsley, chives, sherry, cognac, Worcestershire sauce, salt, and pepper. Cook 3–4 minutes more, stirring well.

4 ▲ Add the cream, and cook another 3–4 minutes, stirring occasionally. Remove from the heat and mix in the egg yolks. Fold in the sautéed scallops.

5 Divide the mixture among 6 greased individual gratin or other baking dishes. Or, if you prefer, put it all in one large shallow baking dish. Dot with the remaining 2 tablespoons of butter or margarine.

6 Bake until bubbling and lightly browned, about 10 minutes. Serve immediately, in the dishes. Garnish with chives, if desired.

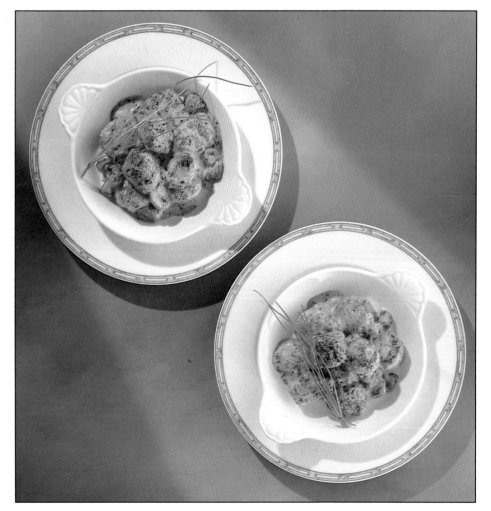

Spaghetti with Clams

SERVES 4

2 dozen hard-shell clams, such as littlenecks, scrubbed
1 cup water
½ cup dry white wine
salt and pepper
1 pound spaghetti, preferably Italian
5 tablespoons olive oil
2 garlic cloves, minced
3 tablespoons minced fresh parsley

1 ▲ Rinse the clams well in cold water and drain. Place in a large kettle with the water and wine and bring to a boil. Cover and steam until the shells open, about 6–8 minutes.

2 Discard any clams that have not opened. Remove the clams from their shells. If large, chop them roughly.

3 ▲ Strain the cooking liquid through a strainer lined with cheesecloth. Place in a small saucepan and boil rapidly until it has reduced by about half. Set aside.

4 Bring a large pot of water to a boil. Add 2 teaspoons of salt. When the water is boiling rapidly, add the spaghetti and stir well as it softens. Cook until the spaghetti is almost done, and still firm to the bite (check package directions for timing).

5 ▼ Meanwhile, heat the olive oil in a large skillet. Add the garlic and cook 2–3 minutes, but do not let it brown. Add the reduced clam liquid and the parsley. Let cook over low heat until the spaghetti is ready.

6 ▲ Drain the spaghetti. Add it to the skillet, raise the heat to medium, and add the clams. Cook 3–4 minutes, stirring constantly to cover the spaghetti with the sauce and to heat the clams.

7 Season with salt and pepper and serve. No cheese is needed with this sauce.

Maine Broiled Lobster Dinner

SERVES 4

4 live lobsters, 1½ pounds each

3 tablespoons minced mixed fresh herbs, such as parsley, chives, and tarragon

1 cup (2 sticks) butter, melted and kept warm

8 ears of tender fresh corn, shucked

salt and pepper

lemon halves, for serving

1 Preheat the broiler.

2 Kill each lobster quickly by inserting the tip of a large chef's knife between the eyes.

3 ▲ Turn the lobster over onto its back and cut it in half, from the head straight down to the tail. Remove and discard the hard sac near the head, and the intestinal vein that runs through the middle of the underside of the tail. All the rest of the lobster meat is edible.

4 ▲ Combine the minced herbs with the melted butter.

5 ▲ Place the lobster halves, shell side up, in a foil-lined broiler pan or a large roasting pan. (You may have to do this in two batches.) Broil about 8 minutes. Turn the lobster halves over, brush generously with the herb butter, and broil 7–8 minutes more.

6 ▲ While the lobsters are cooking, drop the corn into a large pot of rapidly boiling water and cook until just tender, 4–7 minutes. Drain.

7 Serve the lobsters and corn hot, with salt, freshly ground black pepper, lemon halves, and individual bowls of herb butter. Provide crackers for the claws, extra plates for cobs and shells, finger bowls and lots of napkins.

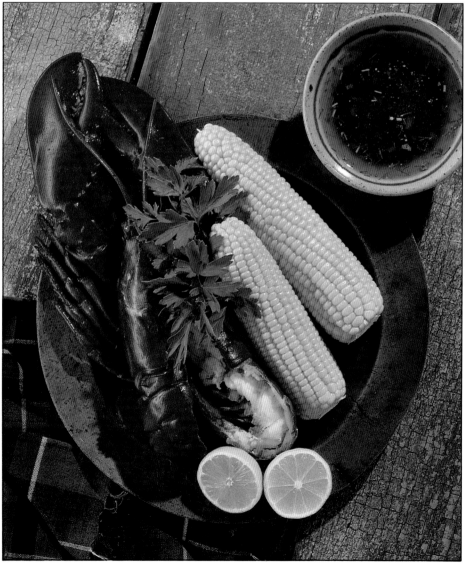

Shrimp Soufflé

SERVES 4–6

1 tablespoon dry bread crumbs
2 tablespoons butter or margarine
⅔ cup coarsely chopped cooked shrimp
1 tablespoon minced fresh tarragon or parsley
¼ teaspoon pepper
3 tablespoons sherry or dry white wine
FOR THE SOUFFLE MIXTURE
3 tablespoons butter or margarine
2½ tablespoons flour
1 cup milk, heated
¾ teaspoon salt
4 egg yolks
5 egg whites

1 ▲ Butter a 6- or 8-cup soufflé mold. Sprinkle with the bread crumbs, tilting the mold to coat the bottom and sides evenly.

2 Preheat the oven to 400°F.

~ VARIATIONS ~

For Lobster Soufflé, substitute 1 large lobster tail for the cooked shrimp. Chop it finely and add to the saucepan with the herbs and wine in place of the shrimp. For Crab Soufflé, use 1 cup fresh lump crab meat, picked over carefully to remove any bits of shell, in place of the shrimp.

---

3 ▲ Melt the butter or margarine in a small saucepan. Add the chopped shrimp and cook 2–3 minutes over low heat. Stir in the herbs, pepper, and wine and cook 1–2 minutes more. Raise the heat and boil rapidly to evaporate the liquid. Remove from the heat and set aside.

4 For the soufflé mixture, melt the butter or margarine in a medium-size heavy saucepan. Add the flour, blending well with a wire whisk. Cook over low heat 2–3 minutes. Pour in the hot milk and whisk vigorously until smooth. Simmer 2 minutes, still whisking. Stir in the salt.

5 ▼ Remove from the heat and immediately beat in the egg yolks, one at a time. Stir in the shrimp mixture.

6 In a large bowl, beat the egg whites until they form stiff peaks. Stir about one-quarter of the egg whites into the shrimp mixture. Gently fold in the rest of the egg whites.

7 Turn the mixture into the prepared mold. Place in the oven and turn the heat down to 375°F. Bake until the soufflé is puffed up and lightly browned on top, 30–40 minutes. Serve immediately.

Chicken Brunswick Stew

SERVES 6

4-pound broiler chicken, cut in serving pieces

salt and pepper

paprika

2 tablespoons olive oil

2 tablespoons butter

2 cups chopped onions

1 cup chopped green or yellow bell pepper

2 cups chopped peeled fresh or canned plum tomatoes

1 cup white wine

2 cups chicken stock or water

¼ cup chopped fresh parsley

½ teaspoon hot pepper sauce

1 tablespoon Worcestershire sauce

2 cups corn kernels (fresh, frozen, or canned)

1 cup lima beans (fresh or frozen)

3 tablespoons flour

biscuits, rice, or potatoes, for serving (optional)

1 ▲ Rinse the chicken pieces under cool water and pat dry with paper towels. Sprinkle each piece lightly with salt and paprika.

2 In a large heavy saucepan or Dutch oven, heat the olive oil with the butter over medium-high heat. Heat until the mixture is sizzling and just starting to change color.

3 ▲ Add the chicken pieces and fry until golden brown on all sides. Remove the chicken pieces with tongs and set aside.

4 ▲ Reduce the heat to low and add the onions and bell pepper to the pan. Cook until softened, 8–10 minutes.

5 Raise the heat. Add the tomatoes and their juice, the wine, stock or water, parsley, and hot pepper and Worcestershire sauces. Stir and bring to a boil.

6 ▲ Return the chicken to the pan, pushing it down in the sauce. Cover, reduce the heat, and simmer 30 minutes, stirring occasionally.

7 ▲ Add the corn and lima beans and mix well. Partly cover and cook 30 minutes more.

8 ▲ Tilt the pan, and skim off as much of the surface fat as possible. In a small bowl, mix the flour with a little water to make a paste.

9 ▲ Gradually stir in about ¾ cup of the hot sauce from the pan. Stir the flour mixture into the stew, and mix well to distribute it evenly. Cook 5–8 minutes more, stirring occasionally.

10 Check the seasoning. Serve the stew in shallow soup plates or large bowls, with biscuits, rice, or potatoes, if desired.

Yankee Pot Roast

SERVES 8

4-pound chuck roast, or bottom round roast or brisket

3 garlic cloves, cut in half or in thirds

½-pound piece of salt pork or slab bacon

2 cups chopped onions

1 cup chopped celery

1½ cups chopped carrots

1 cup diced turnips

2 cups beef or chicken stock

2 cups dry red or white wine

1 bay leaf

1 teaspoon fresh thyme leaves, or ½ teaspoon dried thyme

8 small whole potatoes, or 3 large potatoes quartered

½ teaspoon salt

½ teaspoon pepper

4 tablespoons butter or margarine, at room temperature

¼ cup flour

watercress, for garnishing

1 Preheat the oven to 325°F.

2 ▲ With the tip of a sharp knife, make deep incisions in the chuck roast, on all sides, and insert the garlic pieces.

3 In a large flameproof casserole or Dutch oven, cook the salt pork or bacon over low heat until it renders its fat and begins to brown.

4 ▲ Remove the salt pork with a slotted spoon and discard. Raise the heat to medium-high and add the chuck roast. Brown it on all sides. Remove and set aside.

5 ▲ Add the onions, celery, and carrots to the casserole and cook over low heat until softened, 8–10 minutes. Stir in the turnips. Add the stock, wine, and herbs and mix well. Return the roast. Cover and place in the oven. Cook 2 hours.

6 ▲ Add the potatoes, pushing them down under the other vegetables. Season with salt and pepper. Cover again and cook until the potatoes are tender, about 45 minutes.

7 ▲ In a small bowl, combine the butter or margarine with the flour and mash together to make a paste.

8 Transfer the meat to a warmed serving platter. Remove the potatoes and other vegetables from the casserole with a slotted spoon and arrange around the roast. Keep hot.

9 ▲ Discard the bay leaf. Tilt the casserole and skim off the excess fat from the surface of the cooking liquid. Bring to a boil on top of the stove. Add half of the butter and flour paste and whisk to blend. Cook until the gravy is thickened, 3–4 minutes. Add more of the paste if the gravy is not sufficiently thick. Strain into a gravy boat. Serve with the sliced meat and vegetables, garnished with watercress.

~ VARIATION ~

Add 1½ cups frozen peas to the casserole about 5 minutes before the potatoes are done.

Philadelphia Scrapple

SERVES 10

3 pounds pork neck bones or pigs' knuckles

3 quarts water

2 teaspoons salt

1 bay leaf

2 fresh sage leaves

1 teaspoon pepper

2¾ cups yellow cornmeal

maple syrup, fried eggs, and broiled tomatoes, for serving (optional)

1 Put the pork bones or knuckles, water, salt, and herbs in a large pot. Bring to a boil and simmer 2 hours.

2 ▲ Remove the meat from the bones and chop it finely or grind it. Set aside. Strain the broth and skim off any fat from the surface. Discard the bones.

3 Put 2 quarts of the broth in a large heavy saucepan. Add the chopped or ground meat and the pepper. Bring to a boil.

4 ▲ There should be about 1 quart of broth left. Stir the cornmeal into this. Add to the boiling mixture in the pan and cook until thickened, about 10 minutes, stirring constantly.

5 Reduce the heat to very low, cover the pan, and continue cooking about 25 minutes, stirring often. Check the seasoning.

6 ▲ Turn the mixture into 2 loaf pans and smooth the surface. Let cool, then refrigerate overnight.

7 To serve, cut the loaves into ½-inch slices. Sprinkle with flour and brown on both sides in butter or other fat over medium heat. Serve with warmed maple syrup, fried eggs, and broiled tomato halves, if desired.

Red Flannel Hash with Corned Beef

SERVES 4

6 bacon slices

¾ cup minced onion

2½ cups peeled, boiled, and diced potatoes

1½ cups chopped corned beef

1½ cups diced cooked beets (not in vinegar)

¼ cup light cream or half and half

¼ cup minced fresh parsley

salt and pepper

3 ▼ Heat 4 tablespoons of the reserved bacon fat, or other fat, in the skillet. Add the hash mixture, spreading it evenly with a spatula. Cook over low heat until the base is brown, about 15 minutes. Flip the hash out onto a plate.

4 ▲ Gently slide the hash back into the skillet and cook on the other side until lightly browned. Serve immediately.

1 ▲ Cook the bacon in a large heavy or nonstick skillet until golden and beginning to crisp. Remove with a slotted spatula and drain on paper towels. Pour off all but 2 tablespoons of the bacon fat in the pan, reserving the rest for later.

2 ▲ Cut the bacon into ½-inch pieces and place in a mixing bowl. Cook the onion in the bacon fat over low heat until softened, 8–10 minutes. Remove it from the pan and add to the bacon. Mix in the potatoes, corned beef, beets, cream, and the minced parsley. Season with salt and pepper and mix well.

Boston Baked Beans

SERVES 8

3 cups dried navy or Great Northern beans

1 bay leaf

4 cloves

2 medium-size onions, peeled

½ cup molasses

¾ cup dark brown sugar, firmly packed

1 tablespoon Dijon-style mustard

1 teaspoon salt

1 teaspoon pepper

1 cup boiling water

½-pound piece of salt pork

1 Rinse the beans under cold running water. Drain and place in a large bowl. Cover with cold water and let soak overnight.

2 Drain and rinse the beans. Put them in a large kettle with the bay leaf and cover with fresh cold water. Bring to a boil and simmer until tender, 1½–2 hours. Drain.

3 Preheat the oven to 275°F.

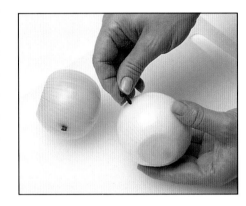

4 ▲ Put the beans in a large casserole. Stick 2 cloves in each of the onions and add them to the pot.

5 In a mixing bowl, combine the molasses, sugar, mustard, salt, and pepper. Add the boiling water and stir to blend.

6 Pour this mixture over the beans. Add more water if necessary so the beans are almost covered with liquid.

7 ▲ Blanch the piece of salt pork in boiling water for 3 minutes. Drain. Score the rind in deep ½-inch cuts. Add the salt pork to the casserole and push down just below the surface of the beans, skin-side up.

8 Cover the casserole and bake in the center of the oven for 4½–5 hours. Uncover for the last half hour, so the pork rind becomes brown and crisp. Slice or shred the pork and serve hot.

Harvard Beets

SERVES 6

5 medium-size cooked beets (about 1½ pounds)

⅓ cup sugar

1 tablespoon cornstarch

½ teaspoon salt

¼ cup cider or white wine vinegar

½ cup beet cooking liquid or water

2 tablespoons butter or margarine

1 Peel the beets and cut into medium-thick slices. Set aside.

2 ▲ In the top of a double boiler, combine all the other ingredients except the butter or margarine. Stir until smooth. Cook over hot water, stirring constantly, until the mixture is smooth and clear.

3 ▼ Add the beets and butter or margarine. Continue to cook over the hot water, stirring occasionally, until the beets are heated through, about 10 minutes. Serve hot.

Boston Baked Beans (top), Harvard Beets

Coleslaw

SERVES 8

1 cup mayonnaise

½ cup white wine vinegar

1 tablespoon Dijon-style mustard

2 teaspoons sugar

1 tablespoon caraway seeds

salt and pepper

8 cups finely sliced green cabbage, or a mixture of green and red cabbage

1 cup grated carrots

1 cup finely sliced yellow or red onions

1 Combine the mayonnaise, vinegar, mustard, sugar, and caraway seeds. Season with salt and pepper.

2 ▼ Put the cabbage, carrots, and onions in a large bowl.

3 ▲ Add the dressing to the vegetables and mix well. Taste for seasoning. Cover and refrigerate 1–2 hours. The cabbage will become more tender the longer it marinates.

Pennsylvania Dutch Fried Tomatoes

SERVES 4

2–3 large green or very firm red tomatoes (about ½ pound)

⅓ cup flour

4 tablespoons butter or bacon fat

salt and pepper

sugar, if needed

4 slices of hot buttered toast

¾ cup half and half

1 ▼ Slice the tomatoes into ½-inch rounds. Coat lightly with flour.

2 ▲ Heat the butter or bacon fat in a skillet. When it is hot, add the tomato slices and cook until browned. Turn them once, and season generously with salt and pepper.

3 If the tomatoes are green, sprinkle each slice with a little sugar. Cook until the other side is brown, 3–4 minutes more.

4 Divide the tomatoes among the slices of toast and keep hot.

5 ▲ Pour the half and half into the hot skillet and bring to a simmer. Cook 1–2 minutes, stirring to mix in the brown bits and cooking juices. Spoon the gravy over the tomatoes, and serve immediately.

~ **VARIATION** ~

For Fried Tomatoes with Ham, top the toast with ham slices before covering with the tomatoes.

Coleslaw (top), Pennsylvania Dutch Fried Tomatoes

Boston Brown Bread

MAKES 2 SMALL LOAVES

1 tablespoon butter or margarine, at
    room temperature

1 cup yellow cornmeal

1 cup graham or whole-wheat flour

1 cup rye flour

2 teaspoons baking soda

1 teaspoon salt

2 cups buttermilk, at room temperature

¾ cup molasses

1 cup chopped raisins

butter or cream cheese, for serving

1 ▲ Grease two 1-pound food cans,
or two 1-quart pudding molds, with
the soft butter or margarine.

2 ▲ Sift all the dry ingredients
together into a large bowl. Tip in any
bran from the whole-wheat flour. Stir
well to blend.

3 In a separate bowl, combine the
buttermilk, molasses, and raisins. Add
to the dry ingredients and mix well.

4 ▲ Pour the batter into the
prepared molds, filling them about
two-thirds full. Cover the tops with
buttered foil, and tie or tape it down
so that the rising bread cannot push
the foil lid off.

5 Set the molds on a rack in a large
kettle with a tight-fitting lid. Pour in
enough warm water to come halfway
up the sides of the molds. Cover the
pan, bring to a boil, and steam 2½
hours. Check occasionally that the
water has not boiled away, and add
more if necessary.

6 Unmold the bread on a warmed
serving dish. Slice and serve with
butter or cream cheese for spreading.

Sweet Potato Biscuits

MAKES ABOUT 24

1¼ cups flour
4 teaspoons baking powder
1 teaspoon salt
1 tablespoon brown sugar
¾ cup mashed cooked sweet potatoes
⅔ cup milk
4 tablespoons butter or margarine, melted

1 Preheat the oven to 450°F.

2 ▲ Sift the flour, baking powder, and salt into a bowl. Add the sugar and stir to mix.

3 ▲ In a separate bowl, combine the sweet potatoes with the milk and melted butter or margarine. Mix well until evenly blended.

4 ▼ Stir the dry ingredients into the sweet potato mixture to make a dough. Turn onto a lightly floured surface and knead lightly just to mix, 1–2 minutes.

5 ▲ Roll or pat out the dough to ½-inch thickness. Cut out rounds with a 1½-inch cookie cutter.

6 Arrange the rounds on a greased cookie sheet. Bake until puffed and lightly golden, about 15 minutes. Serve the biscuits warm.

Boston Cream Pie

SERVES 8

2 cups cake flour

1 tablespoon baking powder

½ teaspoon salt

½ cup (1 stick) butter, at room temperature

1 cup granulated sugar

2 eggs

1 teaspoon vanilla extract

¾ cup milk

FOR THE FILLING

1 cup milk

3 egg yolks

½ cup granulated sugar

¼ cup flour

1 tablespoon butter

1 tablespoon brandy or 1 teaspoon vanilla extract

FOR THE CHOCOLATE GLAZE

1-ounce square unsweetened chocolate

2 tablespoons butter or margarine

½ cup confectioners' sugar, plus extra for dusting

½ teaspoon vanilla extract

about 1 tablespoon hot water

1 Preheat the oven to 375°F.

2 Grease 2 8- × 2-inch round cake pans, and line the bottoms with rounds of greased wax paper.

3 Sift the flour with the baking powder and salt.

4 Beat the butter and granulated sugar together until light and fluffy. Add the eggs one at a time, beating well after each addition. Stir in the vanilla. Add the milk and dry ingredients alternately, mixing only enough to blend thoroughly. Do not over-beat the batter.

5 Divide the cake batter between the prepared pans and spread it out evenly. Bake until a cake tester inserted in the center comes out clean, about 25 minutes.

6 Meanwhile, make the filling. Heat the milk in a small saucepan to boiling point. Remove from the heat.

7 ▲ In a heatproof mixing bowl, beat the egg yolks until smooth. Gradually add the granulated sugar and continue beating until pale yellow. Beat in the flour.

8 ▲ Pour the hot milk into the egg yolk mixture in a steady stream, beating constantly. When all the milk has been added, place the bowl over, not in, a pan of boiling water, or pour the mixture into the top of a double boiler. Heat, stirring constantly, until thickened. Cook 2 minutes more, then remove from the heat. Stir in the butter and brandy or vanilla. Let cool.

9 ▲ When the cake layers have cooled, use a large sharp knife to slice off the domed top to make a flat surface. Place one layer on a serving plate and spread on the filling in a thick layer. Set the other layer on top, cut side down. Smooth the edge of the filling layer so it is flush with the sides of the cake layers.

10 ▲ For the glaze, melt the chocolate with the butter or margarine in the top of a double boiler. When smooth, remove from the heat and beat in the sugar to make a thick paste. Add the vanilla. Beat in a little of the hot water. If the glaze does not have a spreadable consistency, add more water, 1 teaspoon at a time.

11 Spread the glaze evenly over the top of the cake, using a metal spatula. Dust the top with confectioners' sugar. Because of the custard filling, refrigerate any leftover cake.

Shaker Summer Pudding

SERVES 6–8

1 loaf of white farmhouse-type bread, 1–2 days old, sliced
1½ pounds fresh red currants
¼ cup plus 2 tablespoons sugar
¼ cup water
1½ pounds berries: raspberries, blueberries, and blackberries
juice of ½ lemon
whipped cream, for serving (optional)

1 ▲ Trim the crusts from the bread slices. Cut a round of bread to fit in the bottom of a 6-cup domed pudding mold or mixing bowl. Line the sides of the mold with bread slices, cutting them to fit and overlapping them slightly. Reserve enough bread slices to cover the top of the mold.

2 Combine the red currants with ¼ cup of the sugar and the water in a non-reactive saucepan. Heat gently, crushing the berries lightly to help the juices to flow. When the sugar has dissolved, remove from the heat.

3 Tip the currant mixture into a food processor and process until quite smooth. Press through a fine-mesh nylon strainer set in a bowl. Discard the fruit pulp left in the strainer.

4 Put the berries in a bowl with the remaining sugar and the lemon juice. Stir well.

5 One at a time, remove the cut bread pieces from the mold and dip in the red-currant purée. Replace to line the mold evenly.

6 ▲ Spoon the berries into the lined mold, pressing them down evenly. Top with the reserved cut bread slices, which have been dipped in the currant purée.

7 Cover the mold with plastic wrap. Set a small plate, just big enough to fit inside the rim of the mold, on top of the pudding. Weigh it down with cans of food. Refrigerate 8–24 hours.

8 To unmold, remove the weights, plate, and plastic wrap. Run a knife between the mold and the pudding to loosen it. Turn out onto a serving plate. Serve in wedges, with whipped cream if desired.

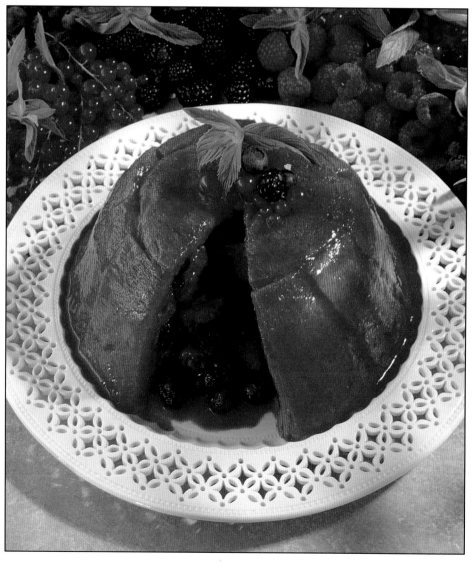

Apple Brown Betty

SERVES 6

1 cup fresh bread crumbs
¾ cup light brown sugar, firmly packed
½ teaspoon ground cinnamon
¼ teaspoon ground cloves
¼ teaspoon grated nutmeg
4 tablespoons butter
2 pounds tart-sweet apples
juice of 1 lemon
⅓ cup finely chopped walnuts

1 Preheat the broiler.

2 ▲ Spread the bread crumbs on a cookie sheet and toast under the broiler until golden, stirring so they color evenly. Set aside.

3 Preheat the oven to 375°F. Butter a 2-quart baking dish.

4 ▲ Mix the sugar with the spices. Cut the butter into pea-size pieces; set aside.

5 ▲ Peel, core, and slice the apples. Toss immediately with the lemon juice to prevent the apple slices from turning brown.

6 Sprinkle about 2½ tablespoons of bread crumbs over the bottom of the prepared dish. Cover with one-third of the apples and sprinkle with one-third of the sugar-spice mixture. Add another layer of bread crumbs and dot with one-third of the butter. Repeat the layers two more times, ending with a layer of bread crumbs. Sprinkle with the nuts, and dot with the remaining butter.

7 Bake until the apples are tender and the top is golden brown, 35–40 minutes. Serve warm. Good with cream or ice cream.

Maryland Peach and Blueberry Pie

SERVES 8

2 cups flour

½ teaspoon salt

2 teaspoons sugar

10 tablespoons (1¼ sticks) cold butter or margarine

1 egg yolk

¼ cup or more ice water

2 tablespoons milk, for glazing

FOR THE FILLING

3 cups peeled, pitted, and sliced fresh peaches

2 cups fresh blueberries

¾ cup sugar

2 tablespoons fresh lemon juice

⅓ cup flour

⅛ teaspoon grated nutmeg

2 tablespoons butter or margarine, cut in pea-size pieces

1 For the pastry, sift the flour, salt, and sugar into a bowl. Using a pastry blender or 2 knives, cut the butter or margarine into the dry ingredients as quickly as possible until the mixture resembles coarse meal.

2 Mix the egg yolk with the ice water and sprinkle over the flour mixture. Combine with a fork until the dough holds together. If the dough is too crumbly, add a little more water, 1 tablespoon at a time. Gather the dough into a ball and flatten into a disk. Wrap in wax paper and refrigerate at least 20 minutes.

3 Roll out two-thirds of the dough between 2 sheets of wax paper to a thickness of about ⅛ inch. Use to line a 9-inch pie pan. Trim all around, leaving a ½-inch overhang. Fold the overhang under to form the edge. Using a fork, press the edge to the rim of the pie pan.

4 ▲ Gather the trimmings and remaining dough into a ball, and roll out to a thickness of about ¼ inch. Using a pastry wheel or sharp knife, cut strips ½ inch wide. Refrigerate both the pie shell and the strips of dough for 20 minutes.

5 Preheat the oven to 400°F.

6 ▲ Line the pie shell with wax paper and fill with dried beans. Bake until the pie shell is just set, 7–10 minutes. Remove from the oven and carefully lift out the paper with the beans. Prick the bottom of the pie shell all over with a fork, then return to the oven and bake 5 minutes more. Let the pie shell cool slightly before filling. Leave the oven on.

7 ▲ In a mixing bowl, combine the peach slices with the blueberries, sugar, lemon juice, flour, and nutmeg. Spoon the fruit mixture evenly into the pie shell. Dot with the pieces of butter or margarine.

8 ▲ Weave a lattice top with the chilled pastry strips, pressing the ends to the baked pie-shell edge. Brush the strips with the milk.

9 Bake the pie 15 minutes. Reduce the heat to 350°F, and continue baking until the filling is tender and bubbling and the pastry lattice is golden, about 30 minutes more. If the pastry gets too brown, cover loosely with a piece of foil. Serve the pie warm or at room temperature.

Brethren's Cider Pie

SERVES 6

1½ cups flour

¼ teaspoon salt

2 teaspoons sugar

½ cup (1 stick) cold butter or margarine

¼ cup or more ice water

FOR THE FILLING

2½ cups apple cider

1 tablespoon butter

1 cup maple syrup

¼ cup water

¼ teaspoon salt

2 eggs, at room temperature, separated

1 teaspoon grated nutmeg

1 ▲ For the pastry, sift the flour, salt, and sugar into a bowl. Using a pastry blender or 2 knives, cut the butter or margarine into the dry ingredients as quickly as possible until the mixture resembles coarse meal.

2 Sprinkle the ice water over the flour mixture. Combine with a fork until the dough holds together. If the dough is too crumbly, add a little more water, 1 tablespoon at a time. Gather the dough into a ball and flatten into a disk. Wrap in wax paper and refrigerate at least 20 minutes.

3 ▲ Meanwhile, place the cider in a medium-size heavy saucepan. Boil until only ¾ cup remains. Let cool.

4 ▲ Roll out the dough between 2 sheets of wax paper to a thickness of about ⅛ inch. Use to line a 9-inch pie pan.

5 ▲ Trim all around, leaving a ½-inch overhang. Fold the overhang under to form the edge. Using a fork, press the edge to the rim of the pan and press up from under with your fingers at intervals for a ruffle effect. Refrigerate 20 minutes.

6 Preheat the oven to 350°F.

7 ▲ For the filling, add the butter, maple syrup, water, and salt to the cider and simmer gently 5–6 minutes. Remove the pan from the heat and let the mixture cool slightly, then whisk in the beaten egg yolks.

8 ▲ In a large bowl, beat the egg whites until they form stiff peaks. Add the cider mixture and fold gently together until evenly blended.

9 ▲ Pour into the prepared pie shell. Dust with the grated nutmeg.

10 Bake until the pastry is golden brown and the filling is well set, 30–35 minutes. Serve warm.

Vermont Baked Maple Custard

SERVES 6

3 eggs

½ cup maple syrup

2½ cups milk

⅛ teaspoon salt

⅛ teaspoon grated nutmeg

~ **COOK'S TIP** ~

Baking delicate mixtures such as custards in a water bath helps protect them from uneven heating which could make them rubbery.

1 Preheat the oven to 350°F.

2 ▼ Combine all the ingredients in a bowl and mix well.

3 ▲ Set individual custard cups or ramekins in a roasting pan half filled with hot water. Pour the custard mixture into the cups. Bake until the custards are set, ¾–1 hour. Test by inserting the blade of a knife in the center: it should come out clean. Serve warm or chilled.

Cranberry Ice

MAKES ABOUT 1½ QUARTS

2 quarts fresh or frozen cranberries

2 cups water

1¾ cups sugar

¼ teaspoon grated orange rind

2 tablespoons fresh orange juice

1 Check the manufacturer's instructions for your ice cream maker, if using one, to find out its capacity. If necessary, halve the recipe.

2 ▲ Pick over and wash the cranberries. Discard any that are blemished or soft.

3 ▼ Place the cranberries in a non-reactive saucepan with the water and bring to a boil. Reduce the heat and simmer until the cranberries are soft, about 15 minutes.

4 Push the cranberry mixture through a fine-mesh nylon strainer set in a bowl. Return the purée to the pan, add the sugar, and stir to dissolve. Boil 5 minutes. Stir in the orange rind and juice. Remove from the heat and let the cranberry mixture cool to room temperature.

5 To freeze in an ice cream maker, pour the cranberry mixture into the machine and freeze following the manufacturer's instructions.

6 ▲ If you do not have an ice cream maker, pour the mixture into a metal or plastic freezer container and freeze until softly set, about 3 hours. Remove the frozen cranberry mixture from the container and chop roughly into 3-inch pieces. Place in a food processor and process until smooth. Return the mixture to the freezer container and freeze again until firm. Repeat this freezing and chopping process 2 or 3 times, then leave to freeze until firm.

Vermont Baked Maple Custard (top), Cranberry Ice

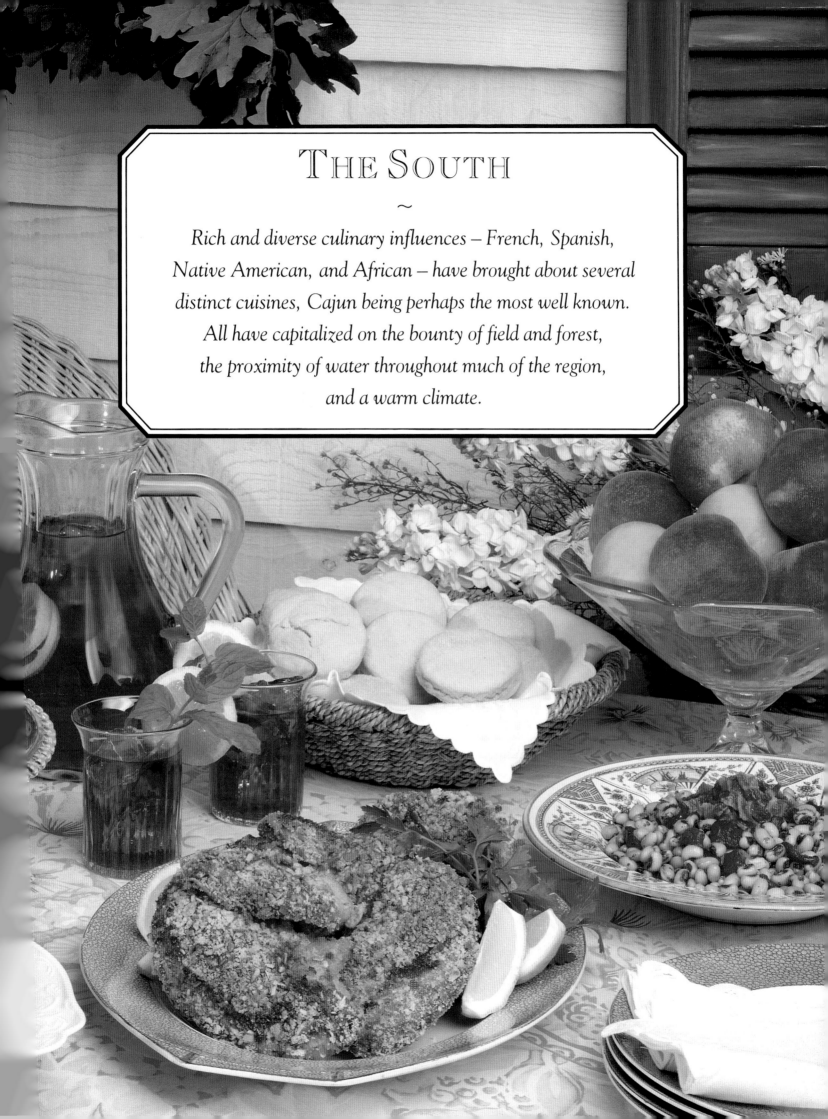

THE SOUTH

~

*Rich and diverse culinary influences – French, Spanish,
Native American, and African – have brought about several
distinct cuisines, Cajun being perhaps the most well known.
All have capitalized on the bounty of field and forest,
the proximity of water throughout much of the region,
and a warm climate.*

Miami Chilled Avocado Soup

SERVES 4

2 large or 3 medium-size ripe avocados

1 tablespoon fresh lemon juice

¾ cup coarsely chopped peeled cucumber

2 tablespoons dry sherry wine

¼ cup coarsely chopped scallions, with some of the green stems

2 cups mild-flavored chicken stock

1 teaspoon salt

hot pepper sauce (optional)

plain yogurt or cream, for serving

1 ▼ Halve the avocados, pull out the pits, and peel. Roughly chop the flesh and place in a food processor or blender. Add the lemon juice, and process until very smooth.

2 ▲ Add the cucumber, sherry, and most of the scallions. Process again until smooth.

3 ▲ In a large bowl, combine the avocado mixture with the chicken stock. Whisk until well blended. Season with the salt and a few drops of hot pepper sauce, if desired. Cover the bowl and chill well.

4 ▲ To serve, fill individual bowls with the soup. Place a spoonful of yogurt or cream in the center of each bowl and swirl with a spoon. Sprinkle with the reserved scallions.

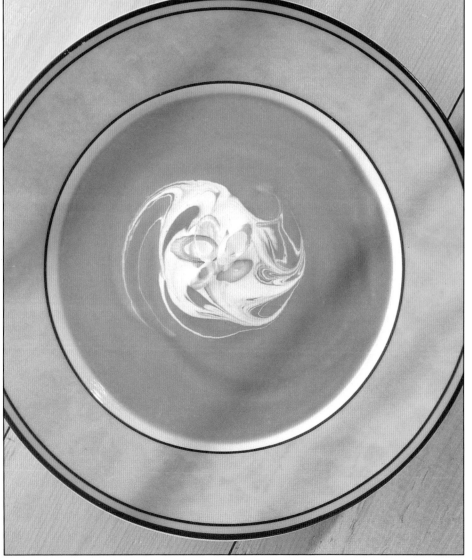

Shrimp and Corn Bisque

SERVES 4

2 tablespoons olive oil

1 onion, minced

4 tablespoons butter or margarine

¼ cup flour

3 cups fish or chicken stock, or clam
   juice

1 cup milk

1 cup peeled cooked small shrimp,
   deveined if necessary

1½ cups corn kernels (fresh, frozen,
   or canned)

½ teaspoon minced fresh dill or thyme

salt

hot pepper sauce

½ cup light cream

1 Heat the olive oil in a large heavy saucepan. Add the onion and cook over low heat until softened, 8–10 minutes.

2 Meanwhile, melt the butter or margarine in a medium-size saucepan. Add the flour and stir with a wire whisk until blended. Cook 1–2 minutes. Pour in the stock and milk and stir to blend. Bring to a boil over medium heat and cook 5–8 minutes, stirring frequently.

3 ▲ Cut each shrimp into 2 or 3 pieces and add to the onion with the corn and dill or thyme. Cook 2–3 minutes, stirring occasionally. Remove the pan from the heat.

4 ▼ Add the sauce mixture to the shrimp and corn mixture and mix well. Remove 3 cups of the soup and purée in a blender or food processor. Return it to the rest of the soup in the pan and stir well. Season with salt and hot pepper sauce to taste.

5 ▲ Add the cream and stir to blend. Heat the soup almost to boiling point, stirring frequently. Serve hot.

Palm Beach Papaya and Avocado Salad

SERVES 4

2 ripe avocados

1 ripe papaya

1 large sweet orange

1 small red onion

2 cups small arugula leaves, washed
   and spun dry

FOR THE DRESSING

¼ cup olive oil

2 tablespoons fresh lemon or lime juice

salt and pepper

1 ▼ Halve the avocados and remove the pits. Carefully peel off the skin. Cut each avocado half lengthwise into 4 thick slices.

2 ▲ Peel the papaya. Cut it in half lengthwise and scoop out the seeds with a spoon. Set aside 1 teaspoon of the seeds for the dressing. Cut each papaya half lengthwise into 8 slices.

3 ▲ Peel the orange. Using a sharp paring knife, cut out the sections, cutting on either side of the dividing membranes. Cut the onion into very thin slices and separate into rings.

4 ▲ Combine the dressing ingredients in a bowl and mix well. Stir in the reserved papaya seeds.

5 Assemble the salad on 4 individual serving plates. Alternate slices of papaya and avocado and add the orange sections and a small mound of arugula topped with onion rings. Spoon on the dressing.

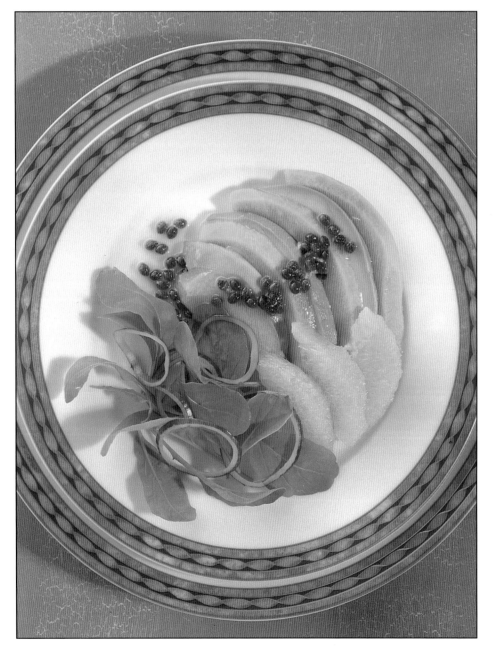

Warm Salad of Black-Eyed Peas

SERVES 4

2 small red bell peppers
½ teaspoon Dijon-style mustard
2 tablespoons wine vinegar
¼ teaspoon salt
⅛ teaspoon pepper
6 tablespoons olive oil
2 tablespoons minced fresh chives
3 cups fresh black-eyed peas
1 bay leaf
8 lean bacon slices

1 Preheat the broiler.

2 ▲ Broil the bell peppers until the skin blackens and blisters, turning the peppers so that all sides are charred. Remove from the broiler and place the peppers in a paper or plastic bag to steam. Let cool 10 minutes.

3 Peel off the skin. Cut the peppers in half, discard the seeds, white membranes, and stem, and slice into ½- × 2-inch strips. Set aside.

~ **COOK'S TIP** ~

If preferred, chop the roasted red peppers rather than cutting them into strips and mix into the warm black-eyed peas.

4 ▼ Combine the mustard and vinegar in a small bowl. Add the salt and pepper. Beat in the oil until well blended. Add the chives.

5 Add the black-eyed peas to a pan of boiling salted water, with the bay leaf. Boil until just tender, 13–15 minutes.

6 Meanwhile, cook the bacon until crisp. Drain on paper towels. Cut or break into small pieces.

7 ▲ When the black-eyed peas are done, drain them and discard the bay leaf. While they are still warm, toss them with the chive dressing.

8 Make a mound of peas on a serving dish. Sprinkle with the bacon pieces and garnish with the strips of red pepper. Serve warm.

Fromajardis

MAKES ABOUT **40**

2 cups flour

¼ teaspoon grated nutmeg

½ teaspoon salt

10 tablespoons cold butter or
    shortening, or a combination of both

6–8 tablespoons ice water

FOR THE FILLING

2 eggs

¼ pound sharp cheddar cheese,
    shredded (about 1 cup)

hot pepper sauce

1 tablespoon minced mixed fresh herbs,
    such as thyme, chives, and sage

1 For the pastry, sift the flour, nutmeg, and salt into a bowl. Using a pastry blender or 2 knives, cut the butter or shortening into the dry ingredients as quickly as possible until the mixture is crumbly and resembles coarse meal.

2 ▲ Sprinkle 6 tablespoons of the ice water over the flour mixture. Combine with a fork until the dough holds together. If the dough is too crumbly, add a little more water, 1 tablespoon at a time. Gather the dough into a ball.

3 ▲ Divide the dough in half and pat each portion into a disk. Wrap the disks in wax paper and refrigerate them at least 20 minutes.

4 Preheat the oven to 425°F.

5 ▲ For the filling, put the eggs in a mixing bowl and beat well with a fork. Add the cheese, hot pepper sauce to taste, and the herbs.

6 ▲ On a lightly floured surface, roll out the dough to a thickness of ⅛ inch or less. Cut out rounds using a 3-inch cookie cutter or drinking glass.

7 ▲ Place 1 teaspoon of filling in the center of each pastry round. Fold over to make half-moon shapes, and press the edges together with the tines of a fork. A bit of filling may ooze through the seam.

8 ▲ Cut a few small slashes in the top of each pastry with the point of a sharp knife. Place on ungreased baking sheets. Bake until the pastries start to darken slightly, 18–20 minutes. To test for doneness, cut one in half; the pastry should be cooked through. Serve warm with drinks.

~ **COOK'S TIP** ~

The fromajardis may be made ahead of time. Let them cool on a wire rack and then store in an airtight container. Just before serving, reheat the pastries in a preheated 375°F oven for 5–10 minutes.

Crab Bayou

1 pound fresh lump crab meat

3 hard-cooked egg yolks

1 teaspoon Dijon-style mustard

6 tablespoons butter or margarine,
    at room temperature

¼ teaspoon cayenne

3 tablespoons sherry wine

2 tablespoons minced fresh parsley

½ cup whipping cream

½ cup thinly sliced scallions, including
    some of the green stems

salt and black pepper

½ cup dry bread crumbs

1   Preheat the oven to 350°F.

2 ▼   Pick over the crab meat and remove any shell or cartilage, keeping the pieces of crab as big as possible.

3 ▲   In a medium bowl, crumble the egg yolks with a fork. Add the mustard, 4 tablespoons of the butter or margarine, and the cayenne, and mash together to form a paste. Mash in the sherry and parsley.

4 ▲   Mix in the cream and scallions. Stir in the crab meat. Season with salt and pepper.

5 ▲   Divide the mixture equally among 6 greased scallop shells or other individual baking dishes. Sprinkle with the bread crumbs and dot with the remaining butter or margarine.

6   Bake until bubbling hot and golden brown, about 20 minutes.

Cajun "Popcorn" with Basil Mayonnaise

SERVES 8

2 pounds raw crawfish tails, peeled, or small shrimp, peeled and deveined

2 eggs

1 cup dry white wine

½ cup fine cornmeal (or all-purpose flour, if not available)

½ cup all-purpose flour

1 tablespoon minced fresh chives

1 garlic clove, minced

½ teaspoon fresh thyme leaves

¼ teaspoon salt

¼ teaspoon cayenne

¼ teaspoon black pepper

oil for deep-frying

FOR THE MAYONNAISE

1 egg yolk

2 teaspoons Dijon-style mustard

1 tablespoon white wine vinegar

salt and pepper

1 cup olive or vegetable oil

½ cup fresh basil leaves, minced

1 ▲ Rinse the crawfish tails or shrimp in cool water. Drain well and set aside in a cool place.

2 Mix together the eggs and wine in a small bowl.

3 ▼ In a mixing bowl, combine the cornmeal and/or flour, chives, garlic, thyme, salt, cayenne, and pepper. Gradually whisk in the egg mixture, blending well. Cover the batter and let stand 1 hour at room temperature.

4 For the mayonnaise, combine the egg yolk, mustard, and vinegar in a mixing bowl. Add salt and pepper to taste. Add the oil in a thin stream, beating vigorously with a wire whisk. When the mixture is thick and smooth, stir in the basil. Cover and refrigerate until ready to serve.

5 Heat 2–3 inches of oil in a large skillet or deep-fryer to 365–370°F. Dip the seafood into the batter and fry in small batches until golden brown, 2–3 minutes. Turn as necessary for even coloring. Remove with a slotted spoon and drain on paper towels. Serve hot, with the basil mayonnaise.

Crawfish or Shrimp Etouffée

SERVES 6

2½ pounds raw crawfish or shrimp in
shell, with heads

3 cups water

⅓ cup vegetable oil or lard

⅓ cup flour

¾ cup minced onions

¼ cup minced green bell pepper

¼ cup minced celery

1 garlic clove, minced

½ cup dry white wine

2 tablespoons butter or margarine

½ cup minced fresh parsley

¼ cup minced fresh chives

salt

hot pepper sauce

rice, for serving

1 Peel and devein the crawfish or
shrimp; reserve the heads and shells.
Keep the seafood in a covered bowl in
the refrigerator.

2 ▲ Put the heads and shells in a
large pot with the water. Bring to a
boil, cover, and simmer 15 minutes.
Strain and reserve 1½ cups of this
stock. Set aside.

3 To make the Cajun roux, heat the
oil or lard in a heavy castiron skillet or
steel saucepan. (Do not use a nonstick
pan.)

4 ▲ When the oil is hot, add the
flour, a little at a time, and blend to a
smooth paste using a long-handled
flat-bottomed wooden spoon.

5 ▲ Cook over medium-low heat,
stirring constantly, until the Cajun
roux reaches the desired color, 25–40
minutes. It will gradually deepen in
color from light beige to tan, to a
deeper, redder brown. When it
reaches the color of peanut butter,
remove the pan from the heat and
immediately mix in the onions, bell
pepper, and celery. Continue stirring
to prevent further darkening.

6 ▲ Return the pan to low heat.
Add the garlic and cook 1–2 minutes,
stirring. Add the seafood stock and
blend well with a wire whisk. Whisk
in the white wine.

7 ▲ Bring to a boil, stirring, and
simmer until the sauce is thick, 3–4
minutes. Remove from the heat.

8 ▲ In a large heavy saucepan, melt
the butter or margarine. Add the
crawfish or shrimp, stir, and cook
until pink, 2–3 minutes. Stir in the
parsley and chives.

9 Add the sauce and stir well to
combine. Season with salt and hot
pepper sauce to taste. Simmer over
medium heat 3–4 minutes more.
Serve hot with rice.

~ **COOK'S TIP** ~

When making the Cajun roux,
take great care not to burn the
flour. If the mixture starts to
smoke, immediately remove the
pan from the heat and stir until
the mixture cools slightly. If the
flour mixture should burn, or if
black specks appear, throw it away
and start again, or the étouffée
will have a bitter burned taste.

Shrimp-Stuffed Eggplant

SERVES 4

2 large firm eggplants, of equal size

2 tablespoons fresh lemon juice

3 tablespoons butter or margarine

½ pound raw shrimp, peeled and deveined

½ cup thinly sliced scallions, including some green stems

1½ cups chopped fresh tomatoes

1 garlic clove, minced

¼ cup chopped fresh parsley

¼ cup chopped fresh basil

⅛ teaspoon grated nutmeg

salt and pepper

hot pepper sauce

½ cup dry bread crumbs

rice, for serving

1 Preheat the oven to 375°F.

2 ▲ Cut the eggplants in half lengthwise. With a small sharp knife, cut around the inside edge of each eggplant half, about ½ inch from the skin. Carefully scoop out the flesh, leaving a shell ½ inch thick.

3 Immerse the shells, skin side up, in cold water to prevent them from discoloring.

~ COOK'S TIP ~

This can also be served cold for an unusual summer dish.

4 ▲ Chop the scooped-out eggplant flesh coarsely, toss with the lemon juice, and set aside.

5 ▲ Melt 2 tablespoons of the butter or margarine in a skillet. Add the shrimp and sauté until pink, 2–3 minutes, turning so they cook evenly. Remove the shrimp with a slotted spoon and set aside.

6 ▲ Add the scallions to the skillet and cook over medium heat about 2 minutes, stirring constantly. Add the tomatoes, garlic, and parsley and cook 5 minutes more.

7 Add the chopped eggplant, basil, and nutmeg. If necessary, add a little water to prevent the vegetables sticking. Mix well. Cover and simmer 8–10 minutes. Remove from the heat.

8 ▲ Cut each shrimp into 2 or 3 pieces. Stir into the vegetable mixture. Season with salt, pepper, and hot sauce to taste.

9 Lightly oil a shallow baking pan large enough to hold the eggplant halves in one layer. Drain and dry the eggplant shells and arrange in the pan.

10 ▲ Sprinkle a layer of bread crumbs into each shell. Spoon in a layer of the shrimp mixture. Repeat, finishing with a layer of crumbs.

11 ▲ Dot with the remaining butter or margarine. Bake until bubbling hot and golden brown on top, 20–25 minutes. Serve immediately, accompanied by rice, if desired.

Shrimp Creole

SERVES 4

1½ pounds raw shrimp in shell, with
   heads, if available

2 cups water

3 tablespoons olive or vegetable oil

1½ cups minced onions

½ cup minced celery

½ cup minced green bell pepper

½ cup chopped fresh parsley

1 garlic clove, minced

1 tablespoon Worcestershire sauce

¼ teaspoon cayenne

½ cup dry white wine

1 cup chopped peeled plum tomatoes

1 teaspoon salt

1 bay leaf

1 teaspoon sugar

rice, for serving

1 ▲ Peel and devein the shrimp;
reserve the heads and shells. Keep the
shrimp in a covered bowl in the
refrigerator while you make the sauce.

2 Put the shrimp heads and shells in a
saucepan with the water. Bring to a
boil and simmer 15 minutes. Strain
and reserve 1½ cups of this stock. Set
the stock aside.

3 ▲ Heat the oil in a heavy
saucepan. Add the onions and cook
over low heat until softened, 8–10
minutes. Add the celery and bell
pepper and cook 5 minutes more. Stir
in the parsley, garlic, Worcestershire
sauce, and cayenne. Cook another 5
minutes, stirring occasionally.

4 Raise the heat to medium. Stir in
the wine and simmer 3–4 minutes.
Add the tomatoes, shrimp stock, salt,
bay leaf, and sugar and bring to a boil.
Stir well, then reduce the heat to low
and simmer until the tomatoes have
fallen apart and the sauce has reduced
slightly, about 30 minutes. Remove
from the heat and let cool slightly.

5 Discard the bay leaf. Pour the sauce
into a food processor or blender and
purée until quite smooth. Taste and
adjust the seasoning.

6 ▲ Return the sauce to the pan and
bring to a boil. Add the shrimp and
simmer until they turn pink, 4–5
minutes only. Serve with rice.

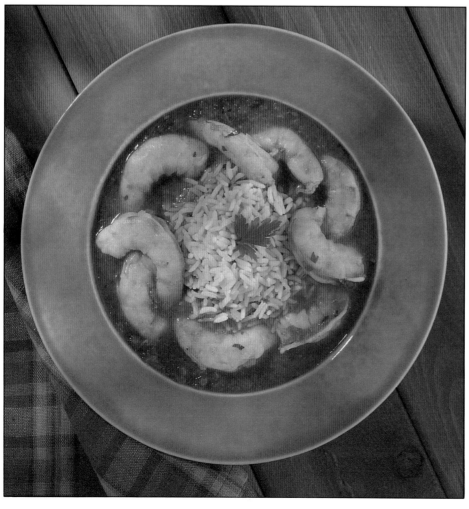

Fried Catfish Fillets with Piquant Sauce

SERVES 4

1 egg

¼ cup olive oil

squeeze of lemon juice

½ teaspoon minced fresh dill or parsley

salt and pepper

4 catfish fillets

½ cup flour

2 tablespoons butter or margarine

FOR THE SAUCE

1 egg yolk

2 tablespoons Dijon-style mustard

2 tablespoons white wine vinegar

2 teaspoons paprika

1¼ cups olive or vegetable oil

2 tablespoons prepared horseradish

½ teaspoon minced garlic

¼ cup minced celery

2 tablespoons catsup

½ teaspoon pepper

½ teaspoon salt

1 ▲ For the sauce, combine the egg yolk, mustard, vinegar, and paprika in a mixing bowl. Add the oil in a thin stream, beating vigorously with a wire whisk to blend it in.

~ **VARIATION** ~

If preferred, serve the catfish fillets with lime or lemon wedges.

2 ▲ When the mixture is smooth and thick, beat in all the other sauce ingredients. Cover and refrigerate until ready to serve.

3 ▲ Combine the egg, 1 tablespoon olive oil, the lemon juice, herbs, and a little salt and pepper in a shallow dish. Beat until well combined.

4 ▼ Dip both sides of each catfish fillet in the egg and herb mixture, then coat lightly with flour, shaking off the excess.

5 Heat the butter or margarine with the remaining olive oil in a large heavy skillet or frying pan. Add the fillets and fry until golden brown on both sides and cooked, 8–10 minutes. To test for doneness, insert the point of a sharp knife into the fish: it should still be opaque in the center.

6 Serve the catfish fillets hot, with the piquant sauce.

Seafood and Sausage Gumbo

SERVES 10–12

3 pounds raw shrimp in shell, with heads, if available

7 cups water

1 onion, quartered

4 bay leaves

¾ cup vegetable oil

1 cup flour

4 tablespoons margarine or butter

3 cups minced onions

2 cups minced green bell pepper

2 cups minced celery

1½ pounds kielbasa (Polish) or andouille sausage, cut in ½-inch rounds

1 pound fresh okra, cut in ½-inch slices

3 garlic cloves, minced

½ teaspoon fresh or dried thyme leaves

2 teaspoons salt

½ teaspoon black pepper

½ teaspoon white pepper

1 teaspoon cayenne

hot pepper sauce (optional)

2 cups chopped peeled fresh or canned plum tomatoes

1 pound fresh lump crab meat

rice, for serving

1 Peel and devein the shrimp; reserve the heads and shells. Keep the shrimp in a covered bowl in the refrigerator while you make the sauce.

2 Put the shrimp heads and shells in a saucepan with the water, quartered onion, and 1 bay leaf. Bring to a boil, then partly cover and simmer 20 minutes. Strain and set aside.

3 Heat the oil in a heavy castiron or steel pan. (Do not use a nonstick pan.) When the oil is hot, add the flour, a little at a time, and blend to a smooth paste using a long-handled flat-bottomed wooden spoon.

4 ▲ Cook over medium-low heat, stirring constantly, until the Cajun roux reaches the desired color, 25–40 minutes. The roux will gradually deepen in color from light beige to tan, to a deeper, redder brown. When it reaches the color of peanut butter, remove the pan from the heat and continue stirring until the roux has cooled and stopped cooking.

5 ▲ Melt the margarine or butter in a large heavy saucepan or Dutch oven. Add the minced onions, bell pepper, and celery. Cook over medium-low heat until the onions are softened, 6–8 minutes, stirring occasionally.

6 ▲ Add the sausage and mix well. Cook 5 minutes more. Add the okra and garlic, stir, and cook until the okra stops producing white "threads."

7 ▲ Add the remaining bay leaves, the thyme, salt, black and white peppers, cayenne, and hot pepper sauce to taste, if desired. Mix well. Stir in 6 cups of the shrimp stock and the tomatoes. Bring to a boil, then partly cover the pan, lower the heat, and simmer about 20 minutes.

8 Whisk in the Cajun roux. Raise the heat and bring to a boil, whisking well. Lower the heat again and simmer, uncovered, 40–50 minutes more, stirring occasionally.

9 ▲ Gently stir in the shrimp and crabmeat. Cook until the shrimp turn pink, 3–4 minutes. To serve, put a mound of hot rice in each serving bowl and ladle on the gumbo, making sure each person gets some seafood and some sausage.

~ **COOK'S TIP** ~

Heavy pans retain their heat. When making a Cajun roux, do not let it get too dark, as the roux will continue cooking off the heat.

Smothered Rabbit

SERVES 4

6 tablespoons soy sauce

hot pepper sauce

½ teaspoon white pepper

1 teaspoon sweet paprika

1 teaspoon dried basil

2- to 3-pound rabbit, cut in pieces

3 tablespoons peanut or olive oil

¾ cup flour

2 cups finely sliced onions

1 cup dry white wine

1 cup chicken or meat stock

1 teaspoon salt

1 teaspoon minced garlic

½ cup minced fresh parsley

mashed potatoes or rice, for serving

1 ▼ Combine the soy sauce, hot pepper sauce to taste, white pepper, paprika, and basil in a medium-size bowl. Add the rabbit pieces and rub them with the mixture. Let marinate at least 1 hour.

2 ▲ Heat the oil in a high-sided ovenproof skillet or Dutch oven. Coat the rabbit pieces lightly in the flour, shaking off the excess. Brown the rabbit in the hot oil, turning frequently, 5–6 minutes. Remove with tongs and set aside.

3 Preheat the oven to 350°F.

4 ▲ Add the onions to the skillet and cook over low heat until softened, 8–10 minutes. Raise the heat to medium, add the wine, and stir well to mix in all the cooking juices.

5 Return the rabbit to the skillet. Add the stock, salt, garlic, and parsley. Mix well and turn the rabbit to coat with the sauce.

6 Cover the skillet and place it in the oven. Cook until the rabbit is tender, about 1 hour, stirring occasionally. Serve with mashed potatoes or rice.

Pork Jambalaya

SERVES 6

2½ pounds boneless pork shoulder butt

¼ cup peanut or olive oil

1½ cups minced onions

1 cup minced celery

1½ cups minced green or red bell
    peppers

1½ cups tasso or other smoked ham,
    cut in ½-inch cubes

1 teaspoon black pepper

1 teaspoon white pepper

½ teaspoon cayenne

1 teaspoon salt

1 garlic clove, minced

1½ cups chopped peeled fresh or
    canned tomatoes

1 bay leaf

½ teaspoon fresh or dried thyme leaves

hot pepper sauce

1 cup dry white wine

2 cups long-grain rice

3–4 cups chicken stock, heated

1 Remove any visible fat or gristle from the pork, and cut the meat into ½-inch cubes.

2 ▲ Heat the oil in a large pot or Dutch oven. Brown the cubes of pork, in batches, stirring to color evenly. Remove the pork with a slotted spoon and set aside.

3 ▼ Add the onions, celery, and bell peppers to the pot and cook, stirring, 3–4 minutes. Add the ham, black and white peppers, cayenne, and salt. Cook over medium heat, stirring frequently, until the onions are soft and golden, about 12 minutes.

4 Add the garlic, tomatoes, herbs, and hot pepper sauce to taste. Cook 5 minutes more. Add the pork and wine and mix well, then cover the pot and cook gently over low heat for about 45 minutes.

5 Add the rice and stir well. Cook 3–4 minutes.

6 Pour in 3 cups of the chicken stock and stir to blend. Bring to a boil. Cover, reduce the heat to low, and simmer until the rice is tender, about 15 minutes. Stir the mixture occasionally and add more chicken stock if necessary. The rice should be moist, not dry and fluffy. Serve from the casserole or in a large heated serving dish.

Pecan-Stuffed Pork Chops

SERVES 4

4 pork chops, at least 1 inch thick, trimmed of almost all fat

½ cup fresh bread crumbs

½ cup minced scallions

½ cup minced apple

½ cup chopped pecans

1 garlic clove, minced

¼ cup minced fresh parsley

¼ teaspoon cayenne

¼ teaspoon black pepper

½ teaspoon dry mustard

⅛ teaspoon ground cumin

2 tablespoons olive oil

½ cup meat or chicken stock

½ cup dry white wine

1 bay leaf

1 Preheat the oven to 350°F.

2 ▲ Make a pocket in each chop by cutting horizontally from the fatty side straight to the bone.

3 ▲ Combine all the other ingredients except the stock, wine, and bay leaf. Mix well. Divide the mixture among the chops, filling each pocket with as much stuffing as it will comfortably hold.

4 ▲ Place the chops in a greased baking dish large enough to hold them in one layer.

5 ▲ Pour the stock and wine over them and add the bay leaf and any leftover stuffing. Cover tightly. Bake until tender, about 1 hour, basting occasionally with pan juices. Serve with cooking juices spooned over.

Ham with Red-Eye Gravy

SERVES 1

1 tablespoon butter or margarine

1 slice of ham, ¼–½ inch thick, preferably uncooked country-style ham, with some fat left on it

½ cup strong brewed coffee, heated

mashed potatoes for serving

~ COOK'S TIP ~

Try ham cooked this way for breakfast, accompanied by grits.

1 ▼ Melt the butter or margarine in a small skillet. Add the ham and sauté until golden brown on both sides. Remove to a warm plate.

2 ▲ Pour the coffee into the skillet and stir to mix with the cooking juices. When the gravy is boiling, pour it over the ham. Serve the ham with mashed potatoes, if desired.

Pecan-Stuffed Pork Chops (top), Ham with Red-Eye Gravy

Oven "Fried" Chicken

SERVES 4

4 large chicken pieces

½ cup flour

½ teaspoon salt

¼ teaspoon pepper

1 egg

2 tablespoons water

2 tablespoons minced mixed fresh herbs, such as parsley, basil, and thyme

1 cup dry bread crumbs

¼ cup freshly grated Parmesan cheese

lemon wedges, for serving

1 Preheat the oven to 400°F.

2 Rinse the chicken pieces in cool water. Pat dry with paper towels.

3 ▼ Combine the flour, salt, and pepper on a plate and stir with a fork to mix. Coat the chicken pieces on both sides with the seasoned flour and shake off the excess.

4 Sprinkle a little water onto the chicken pieces, and coat again lightly with the seasoned flour.

5 ▲ Beat the egg with the water in a shallow dish. Stir in the herbs. Dip the chicken pieces into the egg mixture, turning to coat them evenly.

6 ▲ Combine the bread crumbs and grated Parmesan cheese on a plate. Roll the chicken pieces in the crumbs, patting with your fingers to help them to adhere.

7 ▲ Place the chicken pieces in a greased shallow pan large enough to hold them in one layer. Bake until thoroughly cooked and golden brown, 20–30 minutes. To test for doneness, prick with a fork; the juices that run out should be clear, not pink. Serve hot, with lemon wedges.

Blackened Chicken Breasts

SERVES 6

6 medium-size skinless boneless chicken breast halves

6 tablespoons butter or margarine

1 teaspoon garlic powder

2 teaspoons onion powder

1 teaspoon cayenne

2 teaspoons sweet paprika

1½ teaspoons salt

½ teaspoon white pepper

1 teaspoon black pepper

¼ teaspoon ground cumin

1 teaspoon dried thyme leaves

1 ▲ Slice each chicken breast piece in half horizontally, making 2 pieces of about the same thickness. Flatten slightly with the heel of the hand.

2 Melt the butter or margarine in a small saucepan.

3 ▼ Combine all the remaining ingredients in a shallow bowl and stir to blend well. Brush the chicken pieces on both sides with melted butter or margarine, then sprinkle evenly with the seasoning mixture.

4 Heat a large heavy skillet over high heat until a drop of water sprinkled on the surface sizzles. This will take 5–8 minutes.

5 ▲ Drizzle a teaspoon of melted butter on each chicken piece. Place them in the skillet in an even layer, 2 or 3 at a time. Cook until the underside begins to blacken, 2–3 minutes. Turn and cook the other side 2–3 minutes more. Serve hot.

~ **VARIATION** ~

For Blackened Catfish Fillets, substitute 6 medium catfish fillets for the chicken. Do not slice them in half, but season as chicken and cook 2 minutes on the first side and 1½–2 minutes on the other, or until the fish flakes easily.

Corn Maque Choux

SERVES 4

2 tablespoons peanut or olive oil

½ cup minced onion

⅓ cup minced celery

⅓ cup minced red bell pepper

3 cups corn kernels (fresh, frozen, or canned)

½ teaspoon cayenne

½ cup dry white wine or water

1 medium tomato, diced

1 teaspoon salt

black pepper

3 tablespoons whipping cream

2 tablespoons shredded fresh basil

1 Heat the oil in a heavy saucepan or skillet. Add the onion and cook over low heat until softened, 8–10 minutes, stirring occasionally.

2 ▲ Raise the heat to medium, add the celery and bell pepper, and cook 5 minutes more, stirring.

3 ▲ Stir in the corn kernels and the cayenne and cook until the corn begins to stick to the bottom of the pan, about 10 minutes.

4 ▲ Pour in the wine or water and scrape up the corn from the bottom of the pan. Add the tomato, salt, and pepper to taste. Mix well. Cover and cook over low heat until the tomato has softened, 8–10 minutes.

5 ▲ Remove from the heat, stir in the cream and basil, and serve.

Collards and Rice

SERVES 4

2 cups chicken or meat stock

1 cup long-grain rice

1 tablespoon butter or margarine

½ teaspoon salt

3 cups chopped collard leaves, loosely packed

pepper

1 ▼ Bring the stock to a boil in a medium-size saucepan. Add the rice, butter or margarine, and salt. Stir.

2 ▲ Add the collards, a handful at a time, stirring well after each addition.

3 Bring back to a boil, then cover, reduce the heat, and cook until the rice is tender, 15–20 minutes. Season with pepper before serving.

Corn Maque Choux (top), Collards and Rice

Dirty Rice

SERVES 4

6 tablespoons olive or vegetable oil

1 cup minced onion

½ pound ground pork

1 garlic clove, minced

½ pound chicken gizzards, chopped

½ cup minced celery

½ cup minced red or green bell pepper

½ teaspoon white pepper

1 teaspoon cayenne

1 bay leaf

½ teaspoon fresh or dried thyme leaves

1 teaspoon salt

3 cups chicken stock

½ pound chicken livers, chopped

1 cup long-grain rice

3 tablespoons chopped fresh parsley

1 Heat the oil in a large skillet over low heat. Add the onion and cook until softened, 8–10 minutes.

2 ▼ Add the ground pork. Raise the heat to medium-high and stir with a fork or wooden spoon to break up the lumps. When the meat has lost its pink, raw color, add the garlic and gizzards. Stir well. Cover the pan, lower the heat to medium, and cook 10 minutes, stirring occasionally.

3 ▲ Add the celery and bell pepper and cook 5 minutes more. Stir in the white pepper, cayenne, bay leaf, thyme, and salt. Add the chicken stock, stirring to scrape up the cooking juices in the bottom of the skillet. Cook about 10 minutes, stirring occasionally.

4 ▲ Add the chicken livers and cook 2 minutes, stirring.

5 ▲ Stir in the rice. Reduce the heat to low, cover the pan, and cook until the rice is tender, 15–20 minutes. Stir in the parsley before serving.

Spoonbread

SERVES 4

2½ cups milk

1 cup yellow cornmeal

6 tablespoons butter or margarine

1 teaspoon salt

1½ teaspoons baking powder

3 eggs, separated

1 Preheat the oven to 375°F.

2 ▲ Heat the milk in a heavy saucepan. Just before it boils, beat in the cornmeal with a wire whisk. Cook over low heat about 10 minutes, stirring constantly.

3 ▲ Remove from the heat and beat in the butter or margarine, salt, and baking powder.

4 ▼ Add the egg yolks and beat until the mixture is smooth.

~ **COOK'S TIP** ~

The beaten eggs whites give a light texture a bit like a soufflé.

5 ▲ In a large bowl, beat the egg whites until they form stiff peaks. Fold them into the cornmeal mixture.

6 Pour into a well greased 6-cup baking dish. Bake until puffed and brown, 30–40 minutes. Serve with a spoon from the baking dish, and pass butter on the side.

Charleston Cheese Corn Bread

SERVES 8

¾ cup yellow cornmeal

¾ cup flour

2 teaspoons baking powder

1 teaspoon salt

3 eggs

¾ cup buttermilk

¾ cup chopped corn kernels (fresh, frozen, or canned)

⅓ cup melted shortening or vegetable oil

1 cup shredded sharp cheddar cheese

2 tablespoons butter or margarine

1 Preheat the oven to 400°F.

~ VARIATION ~

For a spicier version, add 1 mild chili pepper, seeded and finely chopped, to the mixture.

2 ▲ In a large bowl, combine the cornmeal, flour, baking powder, and salt. Stir to mix.

3 ▲ In a medium-size bowl, beat the eggs until blended. Stir in the buttermilk, corn, shortening or oil, and ½ cup of the cheese.

4 Put the butter or margarine in an 8- or 9-inch skillet (with a heatproof handle) and place in the oven. Heat until melted. Remove from the oven and swirl the fat around to coat the bottom and sides of the skillet.

5 ▲ Add the liquid ingredients to the dry ones and mix until just blended. Pour the batter into the hot skillet and sprinkle with the remaining cheese.

6 Bake until the bread is golden brown and shrinks slightly from the edges of the skillet, 25–30 minutes. Cut into wedges and serve hot, with butter or margarine.

Hush Puppies

SERVES 6

1 cup flour

2 teaspoons baking powder

1 teaspoon salt

1 cup cornmeal, preferably stone-ground

½ cup minced scallions

1 egg, beaten

1 cup buttermilk

oil for deep-frying

1 Sift the flour, baking powder, and salt into a medium-size bowl. Stir in the cornmeal and the scallions.

2 ▲ In a separate bowl, beat the egg and buttermilk together. Stir rapidly into the dry ingredients. Let the batter rest 20–30 minutes.

3 Heat oil in a deep-fryer or large, heavy saucepan to 375°F (or when a cube of bread browns in 40 seconds).

4 ▼ Drop the cornmeal mixture by tablespoonfuls into the hot oil. If the mixture seems too thick, add a little more buttermilk. Fry until golden brown. Drain on paper towels. Serve the hush puppies hot.

Charleston Cheese Corn Bread (top), Hush Puppies

Cornmeal Biscuits

MAKES ABOUT 12

1¼ cups flour

2½ teaspoons baking powder

¾ teaspoon salt

½ cup cornmeal, plus more for sprinkling

⅓ cup shortening or cold butter

¾ cup milk

1 Preheat the oven to 450°F.

2 ▼ Sift the flour, baking powder, and salt into a bowl. Stir in the cornmeal. Using a pastry blender or 2 knives scissor-fashion, cut the shortening or cold butter into the dry ingredients until the mixture is the consistency of coarse meal.

3 ▲ Make a well in the center and pour in the milk. Stir in quickly with a wooden spoon until the dough begins to pull away from the sides of the bowl, about 1 minute.

4 ▲ Turn the dough onto a lightly floured surface and knead lightly 8–10 times only. Roll out to a thickness of ½ inch. Cut into rounds with a floured 2-inch cookie cutter. Do not twist the cutter.

5 ▲ Sprinkle an ungreased cookie sheet lightly with cornmeal. Arrange the biscuits on the sheet, about 1 inch apart. Sprinkle the tops of the biscuits with more cornmeal.

6 Bake until golden brown, 10–12 minutes. Serve the biscuits hot, with butter or margarine.

French Quarter Beignets

MAKES ABOUT 20

2 cups flour
1 teaspoon salt
1 tablespoon baking powder
1 teaspoon ground cinnamon
2 eggs
¼ cup granulated sugar
¾ cup milk
½ teaspoon vanilla extract
oil for deep-frying
confectioners' sugar, for sprinkling

1 ▲ To make the dough, sift the flour, salt, baking powder, and ground cinnamon into a medium-size mixing bowl.

2 ▲ In a separate bowl, beat together the eggs, granulated sugar, milk, and vanilla. Pour the egg mixture into the dry ingredients and mix together quickly to form a dough.

3 Turn the dough onto a lightly floured surface and knead until smooth and elastic.

4 Heat oil in a deep-fryer or large, heavy saucepan to 375°F.

5 ▼ Roll out the dough to a round ¼ inch thick. Slice diagonally into diamonds about 3 inches long.

6 ▲ Fry in the hot oil, turning once, until golden brown on both sides. Remove with tongs or a slotted spoon and drain well on paper towels. Sprinkle the beignets with confectioners' sugar before serving.

Georgia Peanut Butter Pie

2 cups fine graham-cracker crumbs

¼ cup light brown sugar, firmly packed

6 tablespoons butter or margarine, melted

whipped cream or ice cream, for serving

FOR THE FILLING

3 egg yolks

½ cup granulated sugar

¼ cup light brown sugar, firmly packed

¼ cup cornstarch

⅛ teaspoon salt

2½ cups evaporated milk

2 tablespoons unsalted butter or margarine

1½ teaspoons vanilla extract

½ cup chunky peanut butter, preferably made from freshly ground peanuts

¾ cup confectioners' sugar

1 Preheat the oven to 350°F.

2 ▲ Combine the crumbs, sugar, and butter or margarine in a bowl and blend well. Spread the mixture in a well-greased 9-inch pie pan, pressing evenly over the bottom and sides with your fingertips.

3 Bake the crumb crust 10 minutes. Remove from the oven and let cool. Leave the oven on.

4 ▲ Combine the egg yolks, granulated and brown sugars, cornstarch, and salt in a heavy saucepan.

5 Slowly whisk in the milk. Cook over medium heat, stirring constantly, until the mixture thickens, about 8–10 minutes. Reduce the heat to very low and cook until very thick, 3–4 minutes more.

6 ▲ Beat in the butter or margarine. Stir in the vanilla. Remove from the heat. Cover the surface closely with plastic wrap and let cool.

~ **VARIATIONS** ~

If preferred, use an equal amount of finely crushed vanilla wafers or ginger snaps in place of graham crackers for the crumb crust. Or make the pie with a ready-to-use graham cracker crust.

7 ▲ In a small bowl combine the peanut butter with the confectioners' sugar, working with your fingers to blend the ingredients to the consistency of small crumbs.

8 ▲ Sprinkle all but 3 tablespoons of the peanut butter crumbs evenly over the bottom of the crumb crust.

9 ▲ Pour in the filling, spreading it into an even layer. Sprinkle with the remaining crumbs. Bake 15 minutes.

10 Let the pie cool 1 hour. Serve with whipped cream or ice cream.

Mississippi Mud Cake

SERVES 8–10

2 cups flour

⅛ teaspoon salt

1 teaspoon baking powder

1¼ cups strong brewed coffee

¼ cup bourbon or brandy

5 1-ounce squares unsweetened chocolate

1 cup (2 sticks) butter or margarine

2 cups sugar

2 eggs, at room temperature

1½ teaspoons vanilla extract

unsweetened cocoa powder

sweetened whipped cream or ice cream, for serving

1 Preheat the oven to 275°F.

2 Sift the flour, salt, and baking powder together.

3 ▼ Combine the coffee, bourbon or brandy, chocolate, and butter or margarine in the top of a double boiler. Heat until the chocolate and butter have melted and the mixture is smooth, stirring occasionally.

4 ▲ Pour the chocolate mixture into a large bowl. Using an electric mixer on low speed, gradually beat in the sugar. Continue beating until the sugar has dissolved.

5 Raise the speed to medium and add the sifted dry ingredients. Mix well, then beat in the eggs and vanilla until thoroughly blended.

6 Pour the batter into a well-greased 3-quart bundt pan that has been dusted lightly with cocoa powder. Bake until a cake tester inserted in the cake comes out clean, about 1 hour 20 minutes.

7 ▲ Let cool in the pan for 15 minutes, then unmold onto a wire rack. Let cool completely.

8 When the cake is cold, dust it lightly with cocoa powder. Serve with sweetened whipped cream or ice cream, if desired.

Banana Lemon Layer Cake

SERVES 8–10

2¼ cups cake flour
1¼ teaspoons baking powder
½ teaspoon salt
½ cup (1 stick) butter, at room temperature
1 cup granulated sugar
½ cup light brown sugar, firmly packed
2 eggs
½ teaspoon grated lemon rind
1 cup mashed very ripe bananas
1 teaspoon vanilla extract
¼ cup milk
¾ cup chopped walnuts
FOR THE FROSTING
½ cup (1 stick) butter, at room temperature
4½ cups confectioners' sugar
¾ teaspoon grated lemon rind
3–5 tablespoons fresh lemon juice

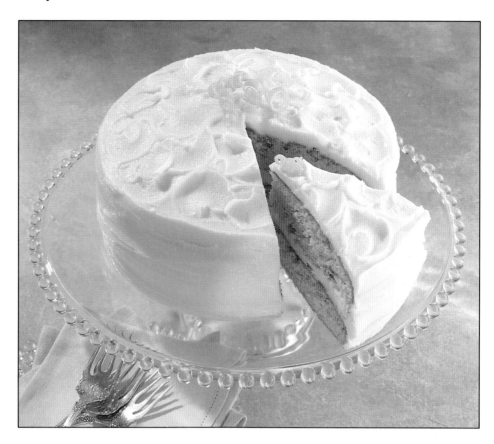

1 Preheat the oven to 350°F. Grease 2 9-inch round cake pans, and line the bottom of each with a disk of greased wax paper.

2 Sift the flour with the baking powder and salt.

3 ▲ In a large mixing bowl, cream the butter with the sugars until light and fluffy. Beat in the eggs, one at a time. Stir in the lemon rind.

4 ▲ In a small bowl mix the mashed bananas with the vanilla and milk. Add the banana mixture and the dry ingredients to the butter mixture alternately in 2 or 3 batches and stir until just blended. Fold in the nuts.

5 Divide the batter between the cake pans and spread it out evenly. Bake until a cake tester inserted in the center comes out clean, 30–35 minutes. Let stand 5 minutes before unmolding onto a wire rack. Peel off the wax paper.

6 For the frosting, cream the butter until smooth, then gradually beat in the sugar. Stir in the lemon rind and enough juice to make a spreadable consistency.

7 ▼ Set one of the cake layers on a serving plate. Cover with about one-third of the frosting. Top with the second cake layer. Spread the remaining frosting evenly over the top and sides of the cake.

Southern Ambrosia

SERVES 6

4 large sweet oranges

1 fresh ripe pineapple

1 coconut

confectioners' sugar (optional)

strips of fresh coconut or lime wedges, for garnishing

1 Using a sharp knife, cut the peel and pith off the oranges, working over a bowl to catch the juices. Slice each orange into very thin rounds and place in the bowl with the juice.

2 ▲ Peel the pineapple. Cut into quarters lengthwise, and cut away the core. Cut into thin slices.

3 Pierce the "eyes" of the coconut with a screwdriver or ice pick. Drain off the liquid. Using a heavy hammer, crack the shell until it can be opened. Prise out the white meat with a blunt knife. Peel the dark brown skin from the coconut meat and shred the meat using the coarse blade of a grater or food processor.

4 To assemble the dessert, layer the fruits and coconut alternately in a glass serving bowl. Sprinkle the layers occasionally with a small amount of confectioners' sugar, if desired, to increase the sweetness. Serve immediately or chill before eating. Garnish with strips of fresh coconut or lime wedges before serving.

Pecan Pralines

MAKES ABOUT 30

1½ cups light brown sugar, firmly packed

1½ cups dark brown sugar, firmly packed

¼ teaspoon salt

½ cup milk

½ cup light cream

2 tablespoons butter or margarine

1 teaspoon vanilla extract

1 cup pecan pieces or halves

~ COOK'S TIP ~

To test for the soft ball stage without a candy thermometer, drop a small amount of the caramel into ice water. It should form a ball that will hold its shape and flatten readily when picked up between the fingers.

1 ▲ In a heavy saucepan mix together the sugars, salt, milk, and cream. Stir constantly until the mixture comes to a boil. Cover the pan and cook, without stirring, until crystals no longer form on the sides of the pan, about 3 minutes.

2 Uncover the pan and cook over medium heat, without stirring, to the soft ball stage, 238°F on a candy thermometer.

3 Remove from the heat and beat in the butter or margarine with a wooden spoon. Continue beating until the mixture is smooth and creamy and the temperature of the mixture comes down to 110°F. Beat in the vanilla and the nuts.

4 ▼ Using 2 spoons, drop the candy by the spoonful onto a baking sheet lined with buttered wax paper. When cool, store the pralines in an airtight container with wax paper between each of the layers.

Southern Ambrosia (top), Pecan Pralines

Pink Grapefruit Sherbet

SERVES 8

¾ cup granulated sugar

½ cup water

4 cups strained freshly squeezed pink
grapefruit juice

1–2 tablespoons fresh lemon juice

confectioners' sugar, to taste

1 In a small heavy saucepan, dissolve
the granulated sugar in the water over
medium heat, without stirring. When
the sugar has dissolved, boil 3–4
minutes. Remove from the heat and
let cool.

2 ▼ Pour the cooled sugar syrup into
the grapefruit juice. Stir well. Taste
the mixture and adjust the flavor by
adding some lemon juice or a little
confectioners' sugar, if necessary, but
do not over-sweeten.

3 ▲ Pour the mixture into a metal or
plastic freezer container and freeze
until softly set, about 3 hours.

4 ▲ Remove from the container and
chop roughly into 3-inch pieces. Place
in a food processor and process until
smooth. Return the mixture to the
freezer container and freeze again until
set. Repeat this freezing and chopping
process 2 or 3 times, until a smooth
consistency is obtained.

5 Alternatively, freeze the sherbet in
an ice cream maker, following the
manufacturer's instructions.

~ **VARIATION** ~

For Orange Sherbet, substitute an
equal amount of orange juice for
the grapefruit juice and increase
the lemon juice to 3–4 tablespoons,
or to taste. For additional flavor,
add 1 tablespoon finely grated
orange rind. If blood oranges are
available, their deep red color gives
a dramatic effect, and the flavor
is exciting as well.

Key Lime Sherbet

SERVES 4

1¼ cups granulated sugar

2½ cups water

grated rind of 1 lime

¾ cup freshly squeezed key lime juice

1–2 tablespoons fresh lemon juice

confectioners' sugar, to taste

1 ▲ In a small heavy saucepan, dissolve the granulated sugar in the water, without stirring, over medium heat. When the sugar has dissolved, boil 5–6 minutes. Remove from the heat and let cool.

2 ▲ Combine the cooled sugar syrup and lime rind and juice in a measure or bowl. Stir well. Taste and adjust the flavor by adding lemon juice or some confectioners' sugar, if necessary. Do not over-sweeten.

3 ▲ Freeze the mixture in an ice cream maker, following the manufacturer's instructions.

4 If you do not have an ice cream maker, pour the mixture into a metal or plastic freezer container and freeze until softly set, about 3 hours.

5 Remove from the container and chop roughly into 3-inch pieces. Place in a food processor and process until smooth. Return the mixture to the freezer container and freeze again until set. Repeat this freezing and chopping process 2 or 3 times, until a smooth consistency is obtained.

~ COOK'S TIP ~

If using an ice cream maker for these sherbets, check the manufacturer's instructions to find out the freezing capacity. If necessary, halve the recipe quantities.

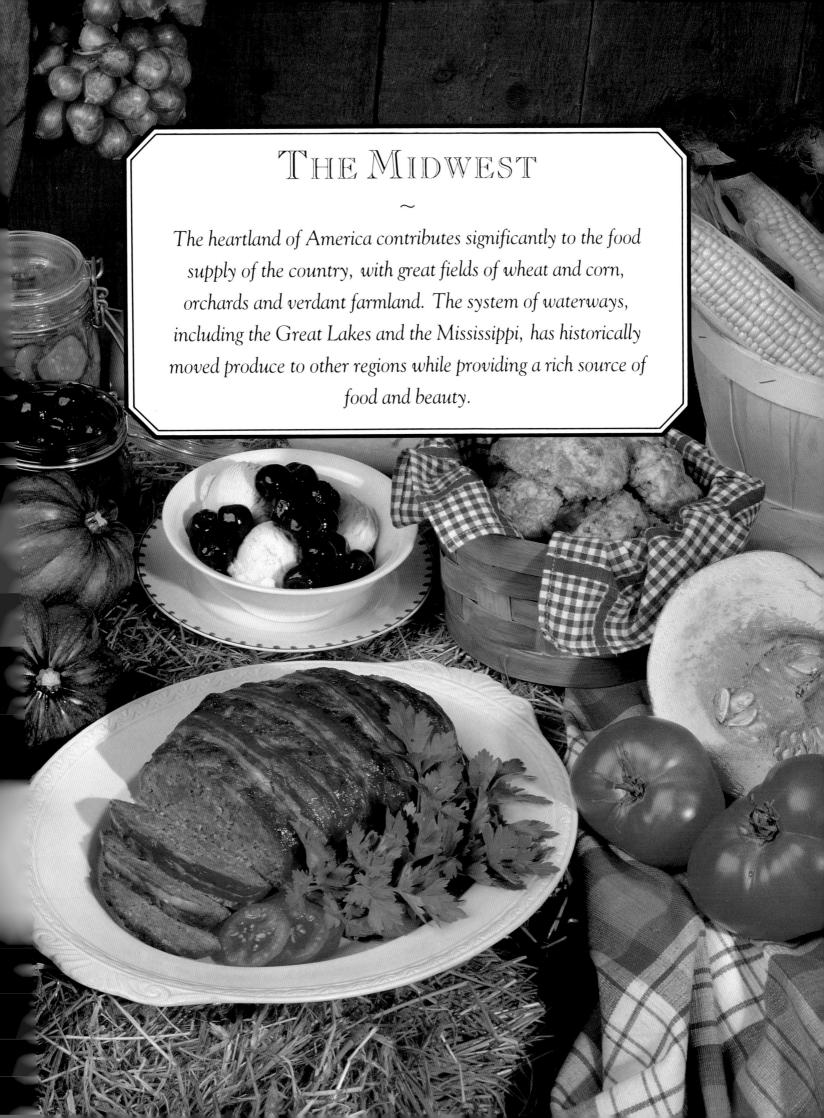

THE MIDWEST

~

The heartland of America contributes significantly to the food supply of the country, with great fields of wheat and corn, orchards and verdant farmland. The system of waterways, including the Great Lakes and the Mississippi, has historically moved produce to other regions while providing a rich source of food and beauty.

Onion Rivel Soup

SERVES 6

4 tablespoons butter or margarine

2 tablespoons olive oil

1½ pounds onions, finely sliced (about 6 cups)

1 tablespoon brown sugar

1 teaspoon salt

2 quarts good beef stock or bouillon, homemade if possible

1 cup dry white wine

FOR THE RIVELS

1 egg

¾–1 cup flour

½ teaspoon salt

pepper

1 Heat the butter or margarine with the oil in a large heavy saucepan. Add the onions and stir to coat well with the fats. Cover the pan and cook over low heat about 15 minutes, stirring occasionally.

2 ▲ Uncover the pan, add the sugar and salt, and continue cooking until the onions turn a rich brown color. Stir often or the onions may burn.

3 ▲ Stir in the stock or bouillon and wine and bring to a boil. Lower the heat and let simmer, partly covered, while you prepare the rivels.

4 ▲ Beat the egg in a medium-size bowl. Add the flour, salt, and pepper to taste and mix with a wooden spoon. Finish mixing with your fingers, rubbing to blend the egg and flour together. The pieces of dough should be pea-size or smaller.

5 ▲ Bring the soup back to a boil. Sprinkle in the pieces of dough, stirring gently. Reduce the heat and simmer about 6 minutes, until the rivels are slightly swollen and cooked through. Serve immediately.

Split Pea Soup

SERVES 8

1 pound dried green split peas
2 quarts water
1 ham bone with some meat left on it, or 1 ham hock
1 cup minced onion
1 cup sliced leeks
½ cup finely sliced celery
¼ cup fresh parsley sprigs
1 teaspoon salt
6 black peppercorns
2 bay leaves

1 ▲ Rinse the split peas under cold running water. Discard any discolored peas. Place the peas in a large kettle and add water to cover. Bring to a boil and boil 2 minutes. Remove from the heat and let soak 1 hour. Drain.

2 ▲ Put the peas back in the kettle and add the measured water, ham bone or hock, onion, leeks, celery, parsley, salt, peppercorns, and bay leaves. Bring to a boil. Reduce the heat, cover, and simmer gently until the peas are tender, 1–1½ hours. Skim occasionally.

3 ▼ Remove the bay leaves and the ham bone or hock from the soup. Cut the meat off the bone, discarding any fat, and chop the meat finely. Set aside. Discard the ham bone and the bay leaves.

4 ▲ Purée the soup in batches in a food processor or blender. Pour into a clean saucepan and add the chopped ham. Check the seasoning. Simmer the soup 3–4 minutes to heat through before serving.

Spiced Pumpkin Soup

SERVES 6

3 tablespoons olive oil

½ cup sliced onion

6 medium-size scallions, bulbs and greens sliced separately

⅛ teaspoon cayenne

¼ teaspoon ground cumin

⅛ teaspoon ground nutmeg or mace

5 cups chicken stock

2½ cups pumpkin purée

½ teaspoon salt

1 cup light cream

1 Heat the oil in a large heavy saucepan. Add the onion and scallion bulbs and cook over low heat until softened, 8–10 minutes.

2 ▲ Add the spices and stir well to coat the onions. Cook 3–4 minutes. Add the pumpkin purée, stock, and salt. Raise the heat to medium; cook 15 minutes, stirring occasionally.

3 Let the soup cool slightly. Purée it in a food processor or blender.

4 ▼ Return the soup to the pan. Taste and add more cayenne if desired. Heat to simmering. Stir in most of the cream and simmer 2–3 minutes more. Serve hot, with a swirl of cream and some sliced scallion greens.

Indian Beef and Berry Soup

SERVES 4

2 tablespoons vegetable oil

1 pound tender steak of beef or buffalo

1½ cups finely sliced onions

2 tablespoons butter

4 cups good beef stock or bouillon

½ teaspoon salt

1 cup fresh huckleberries, blueberries, or blackberries, lightly mashed

1 tablespoon honey

1 Heat the oil in a heavy saucepan until almost smoking. Add the steak and brown on both sides over medium-high heat. Remove the steak and set aside.

2 Reduce the heat to low and add the onions and butter to the pan. Stir well, scraping up the meat juices. Cook over low heat until the onions are softened, 8–10 minutes.

3 ▲ Add the stock or bouillon and salt and bring to a boil, stirring well. Mix in the berries and honey. Simmer 20 minutes.

4 Meanwhile, cut the steak into thin, bite-size slivers.

5 ▼ Taste the soup and add more salt or honey if necessary. Add the steak and its juices to the pan. Stir, cook 30 seconds, and serve.

Spiced Pumpkin Soup (top), Indian Beef and Berry Soup

Dandelion Salad with Hot Bacon Dressing

SERVES 6

¼ pound young tender dandelion leaves or other sharp-flavored leaves such as arugula or rocket (about 2½ cups)

1 head of Boston or leaf lettuce

4 scallions, thinly sliced

8 bacon slices, cut across in thin strips

¼ cup fresh lemon juice

2 tablespoons sugar

1 teaspoon Dijon-style mustard

pepper

1 Carefully pick over the dandelion leaves and wash thoroughly in several changes of water. Pat or spin dry. Wash and dry the lettuce leaves.

2 ▼ Tear each lettuce and dandelion leaf into 2 or 3 pieces. Arrange a mixture of leaves on individual serving plates. Sprinkle with the sliced scallions.

3 ▲ In a small frying pan, cook the bacon until crisp. Remove the bacon pieces with a slotted spoon and drain on paper towels.

4 ▲ Add the lemon juice, sugar, and mustard to the bacon fat in the pan. Heat the mixture gently 3–4 minutes, scraping up the browned bits in the cooking juices and blending in the mustard with a wooden spoon.

5 Spoon the hot dressing over the salads and sprinkle with the bacon pieces and freshly ground black pepper. Serve immediately.

~ COOK'S TIP ~

Commercially grown dandelion leaves are sometimes available from specialist grocers. If picking your own, choose leaves from spring plants that have not yet flowered, and use them fresh. After flowering the leaves of dandelions become bitter and tough.

Vegetable Chili

SERVES 8

¼ cup olive or vegetable oil

2 cups chopped onions

½ cup finely sliced celery

1 cup carrots, cut in ½-inch cubes

2 garlic cloves, minced

½ teaspoon celery seed

¼ teaspoon cayenne

1 teaspoon ground cumin

3 tablespoons chili powder

2 cups canned crushed plum tomatoes with their juice

1 cup vegetable stock or water

1½ teaspoons salt

½ teaspoon fresh or dried thyme leaves

1 bay leaf

2 cups cauliflower florets

2 cups zucchini, cut in ½-inch cubes

kernels from 1 ear of corn

2 cups cooked or canned kidney or pinto beans

hot pepper sauce (optional)

2 Stir in the celery seed, cayenne, cumin, and chili powder. Mix well. Add the tomatoes, stock or water, salt, thyme, and bay leaf. Stir. Cook 15 minutes, uncovered.

3 ▼ Add the cauliflower, zucchini, and corn kernels. Cover and cook a further 15 minutes.

4 ▲ Add the kidney or pinto beans, stir well, and cook 10 minutes more, uncovered. Check the seasoning, and add a dash of hot pepper sauce if desired. Good with freshly boiled rice or baked potatoes.

1 ▲ Heat the oil in a large flameproof casserole or heavy saucepan and add the onions, celery, carrots, and garlic. Cover the casserole and cook over low heat, stirring from time to time, until the onions are softened, 8–10 minutes.

Stuffed Deviled Eggs

SERVES 6

6 hard-cooked eggs, peeled

¼ cup minced cooked ham

6 walnut halves, minced

1 tablespoon minced scallion

1 tablespoon Dijon-style mustard

1 tablespoon mayonnaise

2 teaspoons vinegar

¼ teaspoon salt

¼ teaspoon black pepper

¼ teaspoon cayenne (optional)

paprika and a few slices of dill pickle, for garnishing

1 Cut each egg in half lengthwise. Place the yolks in a bowl and set the whites aside.

2 ▲ Mash the yolks well with a fork, or push them through a strainer. Add all the remaining ingredients and mix well with the yolks. Taste and adjust the seasoning if necessary.

3 ▼ Spoon the filling into the egg white halves, or pipe it in with a pastry bag and nozzle. Garnish the top of each stuffed egg with a little paprika and a small star or other shape cut from the pickle slices. Serve the stuffed eggs at room temperature.

Stuffed Celery Sticks

SERVES 4–6

12 crisp, tender celery stalks

¼ cup crumbled blue cheese

½ cup cream cheese

3 tablespoons sour cream

½ cup chopped walnuts

2 ▼ In a small bowl, combine the crumbled blue cheese, cream cheese, and sour cream. Stir together with a wooden spoon until smoothly blended. Fold in all but 1 tablespoon of the chopped walnuts.

3 ▲ Fill the celery pieces with the cheese mixture. Chill before serving, garnished with the reserved walnuts.

1 ▲ Trim the celery stalks and cut into 4-inch pieces.

~ **VARIATION** ~

Use the same filling to stuff scooped out cherry tomatoes.

Stuffed Deviled Eggs, Stuffed Celery Sticks

Chicago Deep-Pan Pizza

MAKES A 14-INCH PIZZA

1½ packages active dry yeast

1 cup lukewarm water

1 tablespoon sugar

3¾ cups flour

1 teaspoon salt

3 tablespoons olive oil

FOR THE TOPPING

3 tablespoons olive oil

2½ cups diced mozzarella cheese

2½ cups peeled and chopped tomatoes, preferably plum-type

½ cup freshly grated Parmesan cheese

salt and pepper

½ cup fresh basil leaves, loosely packed

1 In a small bowl, mix the yeast with ½ cup of the warm water. Stir in the sugar. Let stand 10 minutes.

2 Put the flour in a food processor fitted with the steel blade. Add the salt. Pour in the yeast mixture, olive oil, and the remaining warm water. Process until the dough begins to form a ball. If the dough is too sticky, add a little more flour. If it will not mass together, add a little more warm water and process again.

3 Turn the dough onto a lightly floured surface. Knead until smooth, about 5 minutes. Form into a ball and place in a lightly oiled large bowl. Cover with a damp dishtowel. Let rise in a warm place until the dough doubles its volume, about 1½ hours.

4 Preheat the oven to 475°F.

5 ▲ Punch the dough down and knead it lightly, 2–3 minutes. Set it in the center of an oiled 14-inch diameter pizza pan. Using your fingertips, stretch and pat out the dough to line the pan evenly.

6 ▲ Prick the dough evenly all over with a fork. Bake 5 minutes.

7 ▲ Brush the pizza dough base with 1 tablespoon olive oil. Sprinkle with the mozzarella, leaving the rim clear. Spoon the tomatoes over the mozzarella and sprinkle with the Parmesan. Season and drizzle over the remaining olive oil.

8 Bake until the crust is golden brown and the topping is bubbling hot, 25–30 minutes. Scatter over the basil leaves and serve.

Pirozhki with Ham Filling

MAKES 12

2 tablespoons butter or margarine

¼ cup minced onions

1½ cups minced cooked ham (about 6 ounces)

½ cup whipping cream

2 tablespoons minced fresh parsley

1 tablespoon Worcestershire sauce

salt and pepper

FOR THE DOUGH

2 cups flour

1 teaspoon salt

2½ teaspoons baking powder

6 tablespoons cold butter or shortening, or a combination of both

¾ cup milk, plus more for brushing

1 ▲ Melt the butter or margarine in a small skillet. Add the onions and cook over low heat until soft and golden, 10–12 minutes. Add the ham and cook 2–3 minutes more, stirring.

2 ▲ Turn the onion and ham mixture into a bowl. Let cool slightly, then stir in the cream, parsley, and Worcestershire sauce. Season with salt and pepper.

3 Preheat the oven to 450°F.

4 ▲ For the dough, sift the flour, salt, and baking powder into a bowl. With a pastry blender or 2 knives used scissor-fashion, cut the butter or shortening into the flour until the mixture resembles coarse meal.

5 Make a well in the center and add the milk. Stir with a fork until the dough begins to pull away from the sides of the bowl, no more than 1 minute. (If overmixed, the pastry will not be as light and tender.)

6 Turn the dough onto a lightly floured surface and knead lightly, less than 1 minute. Roll out to ¼-inch thickness. Cut into 3-inch squares.

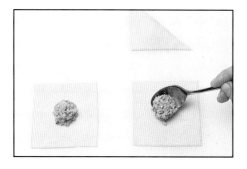

7 ▲ Place a spoonful of the ham filling in the center of each dough square. Brush the edges with milk and fold the dough over to form a triangular shape. Press the edges together with a fork to seal.

8 Arrange the triangles on a baking sheet and brush them with milk. Bake until the pastry is golden and cooked, about 30 minutes.

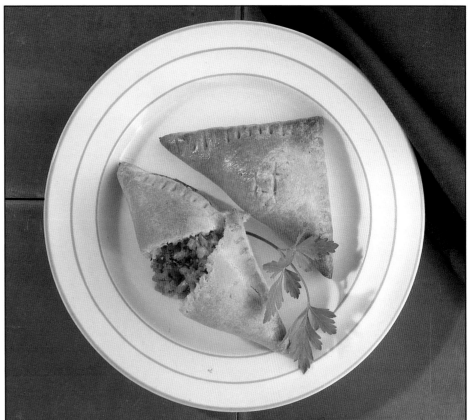

Pan-Fried Honey Chicken Drumsticks

SERVES 4

½ cup honey

juice of 1 lemon

2 tablespoons soy sauce

1 tablespoon sesame seeds

½ teaspoon fresh or dried thyme leaves

12 chicken drumsticks

½ teaspoon salt

½ teaspoon pepper

¾ cup flour

3 tablespoons butter or margarine

3 tablespoons vegetable oil

½ cup white wine

½ cup chicken stock

1 In a large bowl, combine the honey, lemon juice, soy sauce, sesame seeds, and thyme. Add the drumsticks and mix to coat them well. Let marinate in a cool place 2 hours or more, turning occasionally.

2 ▲ Mix the salt, pepper, and flour in a shallow bowl. Drain the drumsticks, reserving the marinade. Roll them in the seasoned flour to coat all over.

3 Heat the butter or margarine with the oil in a large heavy skillet. When hot and sizzling, add the drumsticks. Brown on all sides. Reduce the heat to medium-low and cook until the chicken is done, 12–15 minutes.

4 Test for doneness with a fork; the juices should be clear. Remove the drumsticks to a serving platter and keep hot.

5 ▲ Pour off most of the fat from the pan. Add the wine, stock, and reserved marinade and stir well to mix in the cooking juices on the bottom of the pan. Bring to a boil and simmer until reduced by half. Check for seasoning, then spoon this sauce over the drumsticks and serve.

Oatmeal Pan-Fried Trout

SERVES 4

1½ cups rolled oats

salt and pepper

4 medium-size brook trout, cleaned, heads and tails left on if desired

6 tablespoons butter or margarine

lemon halves, for serving

1 Grind the oats in a food processor or blender until they are the texture of fine meal. Turn into a shallow dish and spread out evenly. Season with salt and pepper.

2 Rinse the trout and dry well with paper towels.

3 Melt the butter or margarine in a large skillet over low heat.

4 ▲ Dip both sides of each trout in the butter or margarine, then roll in the ground oats, patting with your fingers to help the oats stick.

5 ▼ Put the fish in the skillet in one layer. Increase the heat to medium and cook until golden brown, 3–4 minutes on each side. (Cook in batches, if necessary, using more butter or margarine.) Serve hot, with lemon halves on the side.

Pan-Fried Honey Chicken Drumsticks (top), Oatmeal Pan-Fried Trout

Sausage Gravy on Biscuits

SERVES 4

1¾ cups flour

1 teaspoon salt

2½ teaspoons baking powder

4 tablespoons cold butter or shortening

¾ cup plus 3 tablespoons milk

FOR THE GRAVY

3 tablespoons butter or margarine

3 tablespoons minced onion

¾ pound lean bulk pork sausage

¼ cup flour

2 cups milk, warmed

¼ teaspoon paprika

1 tablespoon chopped fresh parsley

1 Preheat the oven to 450°F.

2 For the biscuits, sift the flour, salt, and baking powder into a mixing bowl. Using a pastry blender or 2 knives, cut the butter or shortening into the flour until the mixture resembles coarse meal.

3 Make a well in the center and add ¾ cup of the milk. Stir with a wooden spoon until the dough begins to come away from the sides of the bowl, less than 1 minute. (Do not overmix the dough or the biscuits will not be as light and tender.)

4 Turn the dough onto a lightly floured surface and knead gently about ½ minute, making 8–10 folds only. Roll out to about ¾-inch thickness. Cut out rounds using a 2½-inch cookie cutter. Do not twist the cutter.

5 ▲ Brush the tops of the rounds with the 3 tablespoons of milk. Arrange on a lightly greased cookie sheet. Bake until puffed and lightly golden, 12–15 minutes.

6 While the biscuits are baking, make the gravy. Melt the butter or margarine in a heavy saucepan. Add the onion and cook 3–4 minutes. Add the sausage and cook over medium-low heat until lightly browned and crumbly. Do not overcook. Drain off the excess fat in the pan, leaving about 2–3 tablespoons.

7 ▲ Sprinkle the flour over the sausage mixture in the pan. Stir well to blend thoroughly.

8 Slowly add the warmed milk, blending it in well and scraping up the pan juices. Simmer until thickened. Add the paprika and parsley.

9 Split the biscuits and place on individual serving plates. Spoon the gravy on top and serve immediately.

Twin Cities Meatballs

SERVES 6

2 tablespoons butter or margarine

¼ cup minced onion

¾ pound ground round

¼ pound ground veal

½ pound lean ground pork

1 egg

½ cup mashed potatoes

2 tablespoons minced fresh dill or parsley

1 garlic clove, minced

1 teaspoon salt

½ teaspoon pepper

½ teaspoon ground allspice

¼ teaspoon ground nutmeg

¾ cup fresh bread crumbs

¾ cup milk

¼ cup plus 1 tablespoon flour

2 tablespoons olive oil

¾ cup half and half or evaporated milk

buttered noodles, for serving

1 Melt the butter or margarine in a large skillet. Add the onion and cook over low heat until softened, 8–10 minutes. Remove from the heat. Using a slotted spoon, transfer the onion to a large mixing bowl.

2 ▲ Add the ground meats, egg, mashed potatoes, dill or parsley, garlic, salt, pepper, allspice, and nutmeg to the bowl.

3 Put the breadcrumbs in a small bowl and add the milk. Stir until well moistened, then add to the other ingredients. Mix well.

4 ▲ Shape the mixture into balls about 1 inch in diameter. Roll them in ¼ cup of the flour to coat all over.

5 Add the olive oil to the skillet and heat over medium heat. Add the meatballs and brown on all sides, 8–10 minutes. Shake the pan occasionally to roll the balls so they color evenly. With a slotted spoon, remove the meatballs to a serving dish. Cover with foil and keep warm.

6 ▲ Stir the 1 tablespoon of flour into the fat in the skillet. Add the half and half or evaporated milk and mix in with a small whisk. Simmer 3–4 minutes. Check the seasoning.

7 Pour the gravy over the meatballs. Serve hot with noodles.

~ **COOK'S TIP** ~

The meatballs are also good for a buffet or cocktail party. To serve with drinks, omit the gravy.

Country Meat Loaf

SERVES 6

2 tablespoons butter or margarine

½ cup minced onion

2 garlic cloves, minced

½ cup minced celery

1 pound lean ground beef

½ pound ground veal

½ pound lean ground pork

2 eggs

1 cup fine fresh bread crumbs

½ cup chopped fresh parsley

2 tablespoons chopped fresh basil

½ teaspoon fresh or dried thyme leaves

½ teaspoon salt

½ teaspoon pepper

2 tablespoons Worcestershire sauce

¼ cup chili sauce or catsup

6 bacon slices

1 Preheat the oven to 350°F.

2 ▼ Melt the butter or margarine in a small skillet over low heat. Add the onion, garlic, and celery and cook until softened, 8–10 minutes. Remove from the heat and let cool slightly.

3 ▲ In a large mixing bowl combine the onion, garlic, and celery with all the other ingredients except the bacon. Mix together lightly, using a fork or your fingers. Do not overwork or the meat loaf will be too compact.

4 ▲ Form the meat mixture into an oval loaf. Carefully transfer it to a shallow baking pan.

5 ▲ Lay the bacon slices across the meat loaf. Bake 1¼ hours, basting occasionally with the juices and bacon fat in the pan.

6 Remove from the oven and drain off the fat. Let the meat loaf stand 10 minutes before serving.

Spareribs with Sauerkraut

SERVES 4

3–4 pounds spareribs, cut in
    individual portions

¼ cup minced onion

¼ cup Worcestershire sauce

1 tablespoon dry mustard

½ teaspoon paprika

1 teaspoon salt

3 cups flat beer

3 tablespoons olive or vegetable oil

1½ quarts sauerkraut, canned or bulk

1 tart-sweet apple, peeled, cored, and
    sliced

1 teaspoon caraway seeds

parsley, for garnishing

1 Arrange the ribs in a single layer in a large baking dish.

2 ▲ In a large measure, combine the onion, Worcestershire sauce, mustard, paprika, salt, and beer. Mix well. Pour the mixture evenly over the ribs. Let marinate at least 2 hours, basting occasionally.

3 Preheat the oven to 375°F.

4 Remove the ribs from the dish and pat dry with paper towels. Reserve the marinade.

5 ▲ Heat the oil in a flameproof casserole or Dutch oven. Brown the ribs, turning to sear them on all sides. Work in batches, if necessary. Pour in the marinade. Transfer the casserole to the oven. Bake 35–40 minutes, turning the ribs occasionally.

6 Rinse the sauerkraut, if desired, and drain well. Mix with the apple and caraway seeds.

7 ▼ Remove the pot from the oven. Holding the ribs to one side, distribute the sauerkraut mixture evenly in the bottom of the casserole. Arrange the ribs on top of the kraut, pushing them down evenly.

8 Return to the oven and bake until the meat on the ribs is tender, ¾–1 hour more. Serve the ribs on a large heated platter, on a bed of sauerkraut, garnished with parsley.

Baked Pork Loin with Red Cabbage and Apples

4½-pound boned loin of pork

½ teaspoon ground ginger

salt and pepper

4 tablespoons butter, melted

about 1½ cups sweet apple cider or dry white wine

FOR THE CABBAGE

3 tablespoons butter or margarine

1½ cups finely sliced onions

1 teaspoon caraway seeds

3 tart-sweet apples, quartered, cored, and sliced

1 tablespoon dark brown sugar

3½-pound head of red cabbage, cored and shredded

6 tablespoons cider vinegar, or ¼ cup wine vinegar and 2 tablespoons water

½ cup beef stock

½ cup sweet apple cider or white wine

1 teaspoon salt

¼ teaspoon fresh or dried thyme leaves

1 Preheat the oven to 350°F.

2 ▲ Trim any excess fat from the pork roast. Tie it into a neat shape, if necessary. Sprinkle with the ginger, salt, and pepper.

3 ▲ Place the pork, fat side down, in a large Dutch oven. Cook over medium heat, turning frequently, until browned on all sides, about 15 minutes. Add a little of the melted butter if the roast starts to stick.

4 Cover, transfer to the oven, and roast for 1 hour, basting frequently with the pan drippings, melted butter, and cider or wine.

5 ▲ Meanwhile, to prepare the cabbage, melt the butter or margarine in a large skillet and add the onions and caraway seeds. Cook over low heat until softened, 8–10 minutes. Stir in the apple slices and brown sugar. Cover the pan and cook 4–5 minutes more.

6 Stir in the cabbage. Add the vinegar. Cover and cook 10 minutes. Pour in the stock and cider or wine, add the salt and thyme leaves, and stir well. Cover again and cook over medium-low heat 30 minutes.

7 ▲ After this time, remove the pot from the oven. Transfer the roast to a plate and keep hot. Tilt the pot and spoon off and discard all but 2 tablespoons of the fat.

8 ▲ Transfer the cabbage mixture from the skillet to the Dutch oven and stir well to mix thoroughly with the roasting juices.

9 ▲ Place the pork roast on top of the layer of cabbage. Cover and return to the oven. Cook another hour, basting occasionally with cider or wine.

Spicy Sauerbraten with Gingersnap Gravy

SERVES 8

4-pound beef chuck roast or boneless venison shoulder roast

2 teaspoons salt

pepper

1 cup sliced onions

½ cup sliced carrots

2 bay leaves

1 teaspoon black peppercorns

12 juniper berries

6 whole cloves

1 teaspoon dry mustard

a few blades of mace

2 cups wine vinegar

2 cups boiling water

¼ cup vegetable oil or butter

1 tablespoon dark brown sugar

¾ cup crushed gingersnap cookies

noodles, for serving

1 ▲ Rub the roast with the salt and some freshly ground black pepper.

~ **COOK'S TIP** ~

In braising, meat is browned or seared in hot fat on all sides to seal in the juices before being cooked slowly in liquid. Check the sauerbraten after about 30 minutes of baking to make sure that the cooking liquid is simmering slowly, not boiling. If necessary, lower the oven temperature slightly.

2 ▲ In a deep earthenware crock or non-reactive bowl, combine the onions, carrots, bay leaves, peppercorns, juniper berries, cloves, mustard, mace, and vinegar. Mix well. Stir in the boiling water.

3 ▲ Set the meat in the crock and add more water if necessary: the meat should be at least half covered. Cover tightly and marinate in the refrigerator at least 48 hours and up to 4 days. Turn the meat once a day.

4 Preheat the oven to 350°F.

5 ▲ Remove the meat, reserving the marinade. Pat it dry with paper towels. Heat the oil or butter in a large flameproof casserole and brown the meat on all sides. This will take about 15 minutes.

6 ▲ Add the onions and carrots from the marinade, as well as 2 cups of the liquid. Reserve the remaining marinade. Cover the casserole and transfer to the oven. Cook 4 hours.

7 ▲ Remove the meat to a hot serving platter. Press the vegetables and liquids from the casserole through a fine strainer. There should be about 2½ cups strained liquid; if necessary, add a little more of the marinade liquid. Pour into a saucepan.

8 ▲ Boil until slightly reduced and thickened, about 5 minutes. Stir in the brown sugar and gingersnap crumbs. Adjust the seasoning if necessary.

9 Slice the meat. Serve with the hot gingersnap gravy and boiled noodles, if desired.

Mashed Carrots and Parsnips

SERVES 6

1 pound parsnips, cut in ½-inch slices
    (about 2½ cups)

1 pound carrots, cut in ½-inch slices
    (about 2½ cups)

½ cup chopped onion

1 bay leaf

2 teaspoons sugar

¼ teaspoon salt

1 cup water

2 tablespoons butter or olive oil

minced fresh chives, for garnishing

1 Put the parsnip and carrot slices in a medium-size saucepan with the chopped onion, bay leaf, sugar, and salt. Add the water.

2 ▼ Cover the pan tightly and cook over medium heat, stirring occasionally, until the vegetables are just tender, about 20 minutes. Check from time to time to be sure the water has not evaporated, adding a little more if necessary.

3 ▲ Drain most of the water from the vegetables and discard the bay leaf. Purée the vegetables in a food processor or food mill. Beat in the butter or oil and turn into a warmed serving dish. Sprinkle with the chives, and serve immediately.

Baked Acorn Squash with Herbs

SERVES 4

2 medium-size acorn squash

6 tablespoons mixed minced fresh
    chives, thyme, basil, and parsley

4 tablespoons butter or margarine

salt and pepper

1 ▲ Cut each squash in half crosswise and scoop out the seeds and stringy fibers. If necessary, cut a small slice off the base of each squash half so it sits level.

2 Preheat the oven to 375°F.

3 ▼ Divide the herbs in 4, and spoon into the hollows in the squash halves.

~ **VARIATION** ~

For Caramel-Baked Acorn Squash, replace the herbs with 3 table-spoons dark brown sugar. Melt the butter or margarine, dissolve the brown sugar in it and fill squashes.

4 ▲ Top each half with 1 tablespoon butter or margarine and season with salt and pepper.

5 Arrange the squash halves in a shallow baking dish large enough to hold them in one layer. Pour boiling water into the bottom of the dish, to a depth of about 1 inch. Cover the squash loosely with a piece of foil.

6 Bake until the squash is tender when tested with a fork, ¾–1 hour. Serve hot, keeping the halves upright.

Mashed Carrots and Parsnips (top), Baked Acorn Squash with Herbs

Wisconsin Cheddar and Chive Biscuits

MAKES ABOUT 20

1¾ cups flour

2 teaspoons baking powder

½ teaspoon baking soda

¼ teaspoon salt

¼ teaspoon pepper

5 tablespoons cold unsalted butter

½ cup grated sharp cheddar cheese

2 tablespoons minced fresh chives

¾ cup buttermilk

~ **VARIATION** ~

For Cheddar and Bacon Biscuits, substitute 3 tablespoons crumbled cooked bacon for the chives.

1 Preheat the oven to 400°F.

2 ▲ Sift the flour, baking powder, baking soda, salt, and pepper into a large bowl. Using a pastry blender or 2 knives, cut the butter into the dry ingredients until the mixture resembles coarse meal. Add the cheese and chives and stir to blend.

3 Make a well in the center of the mixture. Add the buttermilk and stir vigorously until the batter comes away from the sides of the bowl, 1 minute.

4 ▼ Drop in 2-tablespoon mounds spaced 2–3 inches apart on a lightly greased cookie sheet. Bake until golden brown, 12–15 minutes.

Corn Oysters

MAKES ABOUT 8

1 cup grated fresh corn

1 egg, separated

2 tablespoons flour

¼ teaspoon salt

¼ teaspoon pepper

2–4 tablespoons butter or margarine

2–4 tablespoons vegetable oil

1 Combine the corn, egg yolk, and flour in a bowl. Mix well. Add the salt and pepper.

~ **COOK'S TIP** ~

Thawed frozen or canned corn kernels can also be used. Drain them well and chop.

2 ▲ In a separate bowl, beat the egg white until it forms stiff peaks. Fold it carefully into the corn mixture.

3 Heat 2 tablespoons of butter or margarine with 2 tablespoons of oil in a skillet. When the fats are very hot and almost smoking, drop tablespoonfuls of the corn mixture into the pan. Fry until crisp and brown on the bases.

4 ▼ Turn the "oysters" over and cook 1–2 minutes on the other side. Drain on paper towels and keep hot. Continue frying the "oysters," adding more fat as necessary.

5 Serve hot as an accompaniment to meat or chicken dishes, or by themselves as a light dish with a mixed salad.

Wisconsin Cheddar and Chive Biscuits (top), Corn Oysters

Milwaukee Onion Shortcake

2 tablespoons butter or olive oil

2½ cups thinly sliced onions

½ teaspoon salt

½ teaspoon fresh or dried thyme leaves

¼ teaspoon pepper

1 egg

½ cup sour cream or plain yogurt

2 teaspoons poppy seeds

¼ teaspoon ground mace or nutmeg

FOR THE SHORTCAKE DOUGH

1 cup flour

1¼ teaspoons baking powder

½ teaspoon salt

3 tablespoons cold butter or shortening

6 tablespoons milk

1 ▲ Heat the butter or oil in a medium-size skillet. Add the onions and cook over low heat until soft and golden, 10–12 minutes. Season with the salt, thyme, and pepper. Remove from the heat and let cool.

2 Preheat the oven to 425°F.

3 ▲ For the shortcake dough, sift the flour, baking powder, and salt into a bowl. Using a pastry blender or 2 knives, cut the butter or shortening into the dry ingredients until the mixture resembles coarse meal. Add the milk and stir in lightly with a wooden spoon to make a dough.

4 Turn the dough onto a floured surface and knead lightly, ½ minute.

5 Pat out the dough into a disk about 8 inches in diameter. Transfer to an 8-inch baking pan that is at least 2 inches deep. Press the dough into an even layer. Cover with the onions.

6 ▲ Beat together the egg and sour cream or yogurt. Spread evenly over the onions. Sprinkle with the poppy seeds and mace or nutmeg. Bake until the egg topping is puffed and golden, 25–30 minutes.

7 Let cool in the pan 10 minutes. Slip a knife between the shortcake and the pan to loosen, then unmold onto a plate. Cut the shortcake into wedges and serve warm.

Huckleberry Coffee Cake

SERVES 10

2 cups flour

1 tablespoon baking powder

1 teaspoon salt

⅓ cup butter or margarine, at room
    temperature

¾ cup granulated sugar

1 egg

1 cup milk

½ teaspoon grated lemon rind

2 cups fresh or frozen huckleberries,
    well drained

1 cup confectioners' sugar

2 tablespoons fresh lemon juice

1 Preheat the oven to 350°F.

2 ▲ Sift the flour with the baking
powder and salt.

3 ▲ In a large bowl, beat the butter
or margarine with the granulated sugar
until light and fluffy. Beat in the egg
and milk. Fold in the flour mixture,
mixing well until evenly blended to a
batter. Mix in the lemon rind.

4 ▼ Spread half of the batter in a
greased 13- × 9- × 2-inch baking
pan. Sprinkle with 1 cup of the
berries. Top with the remaining batter
and sprinkle with the rest of the
berries. Bake until golden brown and a
cake tester inserted in the center
comes out clean, 35–45 minutes.

5 ▲ Mix the confectioners' sugar
gradually into the lemon juice to make
a smooth glaze with a pourable
consistency. Drizzle the glaze over the
top of the warm coffee cake and allow
it to set before serving, still warm or at
room temperature.

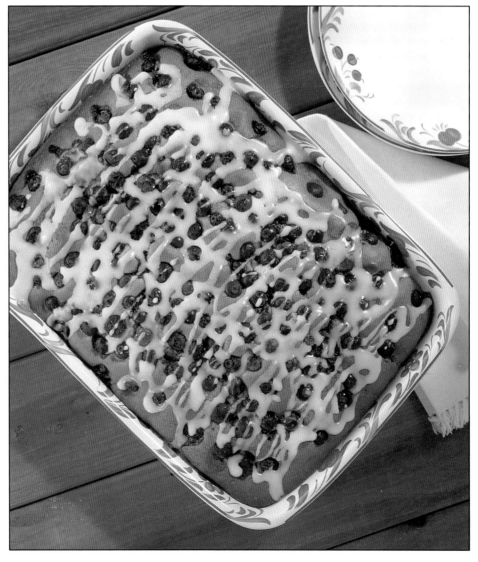

Pickled Eggs and Beets

SERVES 8

2 pounds small beets, cooked and peeled

1½ cups cider vinegar

1½ cups beet cooking liquid or water

½ cup sugar

1 bay leaf

1 teaspoon salt

1 tablespoon whole allspice berries

1 teaspoon whole cloves

½ teaspoon ground ginger

½ teaspoon caraway seeds

8 hard-cooked eggs, shelled

1 ▲ Place the beets in a very large glass jar, or in several smaller jars.

2 Combine the vinegar, beet liquid or water, sugar, bay leaf, salt, and spices in a saucepan. Heat, stirring to dissolve the sugar. Simmer 5 minutes.

3 Pour the mixture over the beets. Let cool completely.

4 ▼ Add the eggs to the jar of beets. Cover and refrigerate 2 or 3 days before serving. The pickle will keep up to a week in the refrigerator.

Bread and Butter Pickles

MAKES ABOUT 4 CUPS

2 pounds cucumbers, scrubbed and cut in ¼-inch slices

2 cups very thinly sliced onions

2 tablespoons salt

1½ cups cider vinegar

1½ cups sugar

2 tablespoons mustard seeds

2 tablespoons celery seeds

¼ teaspoon turmeric

¼ teaspoon cayenne

1 ▲ Put the sliced cucumbers and onions in a large bowl and sprinkle with the salt. Mix well. Cover loosely and let stand 3 hours.

2 Drain the vegetables. Rinse well under cold water and drain again.

3 Prepare some heatproof glass jars (such as canning jars). Wash them well in warm soapy water and rinse thoroughly in clean warm water. Put them in a 300°F oven and heat 30 minutes to sterilize them. Keep the jars hot until ready to use.

4 ▼ Combine the remaining ingredients in a large non-reactive saucepan and bring to a boil. Add the cucumbers and onions. Reduce the heat and simmer 2–3 minutes. Do not boil or the pickles will be limp.

5 ▲ Spoon the hot vegetables into the hot jars. Add enough of the hot liquid to come to ½ inch from the top. Carefully wipe the jar rims with a clean damp cloth.

6 To seal, cover the surface of the pickles with a waxed disc, wax side down, then put on the jar lid. The pickles should be sealed immediately. If the lid does not have a rubber gasket, first cover the top of the jar with plastic wrap or cellophane and then screw a plastic top down over it. Avoid using metal, as it may rust. Store in a cool dark place at least 4 weeks before serving.

Pickled Eggs and Beets, Bread and Butter Pickles

Rhubarb Pie

SERVES 6

1½ cups flour
½ teaspoon salt
2 teaspoons sugar
6 tablespoons cold butter or shortening
¼ cup or more ice water
2 tablespoons whipping cream
FOR THE FILLING
3½ cups fresh rhubarb, cut in ½- to 1-inch slices (about 2 pounds)
2 tablespoons cornstarch
1 egg
1½ cups sugar
1 tablespoon grated orange rind

1 ▲ For the pastry, sift the flour, salt, and sugar into a bowl. Using a pastry blender or 2 knives, cut the butter or shortening into the dry ingredients as quickly as possible until the mixture resembles coarse meal.

2 Sprinkle with the ice water and mix until the dough holds together. If the dough is too crumbly, add a little more water, 1 tablespoon at a time.

~ **COOK'S TIP** ~

Be sure to cut off and discard the green rhubarb leaves from the pink stalks, as they are toxic and not edible.

3 ▲ Gather the dough into a ball, flatten into a disk, wrap in wax paper, and refrigerate at least 20 minutes.

4 ▲ Roll out the dough between 2 sheets of wax paper to a thickness of about ⅛ inch. Use to line a 9-inch pie pan. Trim all around, leaving a ½-inch overhang. Fold the overhang under the edge and flute. Refrigerate the pie shell and dough trimmings 30 minutes.

5 ▲ For the filling, put the rhubarb in a bowl and sprinkle with the cornstarch. Toss to coat.

6 Preheat the oven to 425°F.

7 In a small bowl beat the egg with the sugar. Mix in the orange rind.

8 ▲ Stir the sugar mixture into the rhubarb and mix well. Spoon the fruit into the pie shell.

9 ▲ Roll out the dough trimmings. Stamp out decorative shapes with a cookie cutter or cut shapes with a small knife, using a cardboard template as a guide, if wished.

10 Arrange the shapes on top of the pie. Brush the trimmings and the edge of the pie shell with cream.

11 Bake 30 minutes. Reduce the heat to 325°F and continue baking until the pastry is golden brown and the rhubarb is tender, about 15–20 minutes more.

Brown Sugar Pie

SERVES 8

1½ cups flour

½ teaspoon salt

2 teaspoons granulated sugar

6 tablespoons cold butter

¼ cup or more ice water

FOR THE FILLING

¼ cup flour, sifted

1 cup light brown sugar

½ teaspoon vanilla extract

1½ cups whipping cream

3 tablespoons butter, cut in tiny pieces

⅛ teaspoon grated nutmeg

1 Sift the flour, salt, and sugar into a bowl. Using a pastry blender or 2 knives, cut in the butter until it resembles coarse meal.

2 ▲ Sprinkle with the water and mix until the dough holds together. If it is too crumbly, add more water, 1 tablespoon at a time. Gather into a ball and flatten. Wrap in wax paper and refrigerate at least 20 minutes.

3 Roll out the dough about ⅛ inch thick and line a 9-inch pie pan. Trim all around, leaving a ½-inch overhang. Fold it under and flute the edge. Refrigerate for 30 minutes.

4 Preheat the oven to 425°F.

5 Line the pie shell with a piece of wax paper that is 2 inches larger all around than the diameter of the pan. Fill the shell with dried beans. Bake until the pastry has just set, 8–10 minutes. Remove from the oven and carefully lift out the paper and beans. Prick the bottom of the pie shell all over with a fork. Return to the oven and bake 5 minutes more. Let the pie shell cool slightly before filling. Turn the oven down to 375°F.

6 ▲ In a small bowl, mix together the flour and sugar using a fork. Spread this mixture in an even layer on the bottom of the pie shell.

7 ▲ Stir the vanilla into the cream. Pour the flavored cream over the flour and sugar mixture and gently swirl with a fork to mix. Dot with the butter. Sprinkle the nutmeg on top.

8 Cover the edge of the pie with foil strips to prevent overbrowning. Set on a cookie sheet and bake until the filling is golden brown and set to the touch, about 45 minutes. Serve the pie at room temperature.

Apple Maple Dumplings

SERVES 8

4½ cups flour
2 teaspoons salt
1½ cups shortening
¾–1 cup ice water
8 firm, tart-sweet apples
1 egg white
⅔ cup sugar
3 tablespoons whipping cream
½ teaspoon vanilla extract
1 cup maple syrup
whipped cream, for serving

1 Sift the flour and salt into a large bowl. Using a pastry blender or 2 knives, cut in the shortening until the mixture resembles coarse meal. Sprinkle with ¾ cup water and mix until the dough holds together. If it is too crumbly, add a little more water. Gather into a ball. Wrap in wax paper and refrigerate at least 20 minutes.

2 Preheat the oven to 425°F.

3 Peel the apples. Remove the cores, cutting from the stem end, without cutting through the base.

4 ▲ Roll out the dough thinly. Cut squares almost large enough to enclose the apples. Brush the squares with egg white. Set an apple in the center of each square of dough.

5 Combine the sugar, cream, and vanilla in a small bowl. Spoon some into the hollow in each apple.

6 ▼ Pull the points of the dough squares up around the apples and moisten the edges where they overlap. Mold the dough around the apples, pleating the top. Do not cover the center hollows. Crimp the edges tightly to seal.

7 Set the apples in a large greased baking dish, at least ¾ inch apart. Bake 30 minutes. Lower the oven temperature to 350°F and continue baking until the pastry is golden brown and the apples are tender, about 20 minutes more.

8 Transfer the dumplings to a serving dish. Mix the maple syrup with the juices in the baking dish and drizzle over the dumplings.

9 Serve the dumplings hot with whipped cream.

Apple Fritters

Serves 4–6

1⅓ cups flour

2 teaspoons baking powder

¼ teaspoon salt

⅔ cup milk

1 egg, beaten

oil for deep-frying

¾ cup granulated sugar

1 teaspoon ground cinnamon

2 large tart-sweet apples, peeled, cored, and cut in ¼-inch slices

confectioners' sugar, for dusting

1 Sift the flour, baking powder, and salt into a bowl. Beat in the milk and egg with a wire whisk.

2 Heat at least 3 inches of oil in a heavy frying pan to 360°F.

3 ▲ Mix the granulated sugar and cinnamon in a shallow bowl or plate. Toss the apple slices in the sugar mixture to coat all over.

4 Dip the apple slices in the batter, using a fork or slotted spoon. Drain off excess batter. Fry, in batches, in the hot oil until golden brown on both sides, about 4–5 minutes. Drain the fritters on paper towels.

5 ▼ Sprinkle with confectioners' sugar, and serve hot.

Cherry Compote

Serves 6

½ cup water

½ cup red wine

¼ cup light brown sugar, firmly packed

¼ cup granulated sugar

1 tablespoon honey

2 1-inch strips of orange rind

¼ teaspoon almond extract

1½ pounds sweet fresh cherries, pitted

ice cream or whipped cream, for serving

~ VARIATION ~

Sour cherries may be used for the compote instead of sweet. If using sour cherries, increase the amount of the sugars to ⅓ cup each, or to taste.

---

1 ▼ Combine all the ingredients except the cherries in a saucepan. Stir over medium heat until the sugar dissolves. Raise the heat and boil until the liquid reduces slightly.

2 ▲ Add the cherries. Bring back to a boil. Reduce the heat slightly and simmer 8–10 minutes. If necessary, skim off any foam.

3 Let cool to lukewarm. Spoon warm over vanilla ice cream, or refrigerate and serve cold with whipped cream, if desired.

Apple Fritters (top), Cherry Compote

Black Walnut Layer Cake

SERVES 8

2 cups cake flour
1 tablespoon baking powder
½ teaspoon salt
½ cup (1 stick) butter or margarine, at room temperature
1 cup granulated sugar
2 eggs
1 teaspoon grated orange rind
1 teaspoon vanilla extract
1 cup minced black walnut pieces
¾ cup milk
black walnut halves, for decoration

FOR THE FROSTING

½ cup (1 stick) butter
¾ cup light brown sugar, firmly packed
3 tablespoons maple syrup
¼ cup milk
1¾–2 cups confectioners' sugar, sifted

1 ▲ Grease 2 8- × 2-inch cake pans and line the bottoms of each with a disk of greased wax paper. Preheat the oven to 375°F.

2 Sift together the flour, baking powder, and salt.

~ **VARIATION** ~

If black walnuts are unavailable, substitute regular walnuts, or use pecans instead.

3 ▲ Beat the butter or margarine to soften, then gradually beat in the granulated sugar until light and fluffy. Beat in the eggs, one at a time. Add the orange rind and vanilla and beat to mix well.

4 ▲ Stir in the minced walnuts. Add the flour alternately with the milk, stirring only enough to blend after each addition.

5 ▲ Divide the batter between the prepared cake pans. Bake until a cake tester inserted in the center comes out clean, about 25 minutes. Cool in the cake pans for 5 minutes before unmolding onto a wire rack.

6 ▲ For the frosting, melt the butter in a medium-size saucepan. Add the brown sugar and maple syrup and boil 2 minutes, stirring constantly.

7 ▲ Add the milk. Bring back to a boil and stir in ¼ cup of the confectioners' sugar. Remove from the heat and let cool to lukewarm. Gradually beat in the remaining confectioners' sugar. Set the pan in a bowl of ice water and stir until the frosting is thick enough to spread.

8 ▲ Spread some of the frosting on one of the cake layers. Set the other layer on top. Spread the remaining frosting over the top and sides of the cake. Decorate with walnut halves.

Applesauce Cookies

MAKES 3 DOZEN

½ cup sugar

4 tablespoons butter or shortening, at room temperature

¾ cup thick applesauce

⅛ teaspoon grated lemon rind

1 cup flour

½ teaspoon baking powder

¼ teaspoon baking soda

¼ teaspoon salt

½ teaspoon ground cinnamon

½ cup chopped walnuts

```
~ COOK'S TIP ~

If the applesauce is runny, put it
in a strainer over a bowl and let it
drain for 10 minutes.
```

1 Preheat the oven to 375°F.

2 In a medium-size bowl, beat together the sugar and butter or shortening until well mixed. Beat in the applesauce and lemon rind.

3 ▲ Sift the flour, baking powder, baking soda, salt, and cinnamon into the mixture, and stir to blend. Fold in the chopped walnuts.

4 ▲ Drop teaspoonfuls of the dough on a lightly greased cookie sheet, spacing them about 2 inches apart.

5 Bake the cookies in the center of the oven until they are golden brown, 8–10 minutes. Transfer the cookies to a wire rack to cool.

Toffee Bars

MAKES 32

2 cups light brown sugar, firmly packed

2 cups (4 sticks) butter or margarine, at room temperature

2 egg yolks

1½ teaspoons vanilla extract

4 cups all-purpose or whole-wheat flour

½ teaspoon salt

2 4-ounce bars of milk chocolate, broken in pieces

1 cup chopped walnuts or pecans

1 Preheat the oven to 350°F.

2 Beat together the sugar and butter or margarine until light and fluffy. Beat in the egg yolks and vanilla. Stir in the flour and salt.

3 ▼ Spread the dough in a greased 13- × 9- × 2-inch baking pan. Bake until lightly browned, 25–30 minutes. The texture will be soft.

4 ▲ Remove from the oven and immediately place the chocolate pieces on the hot cookie base. Let stand until the chocolate softens, then spread it evenly with a spatula. Sprinkle with the nuts.

5 While still warm, cut into bars about 2 × 1½ inches.

Applesauce Cookies (top), Toffee Bars

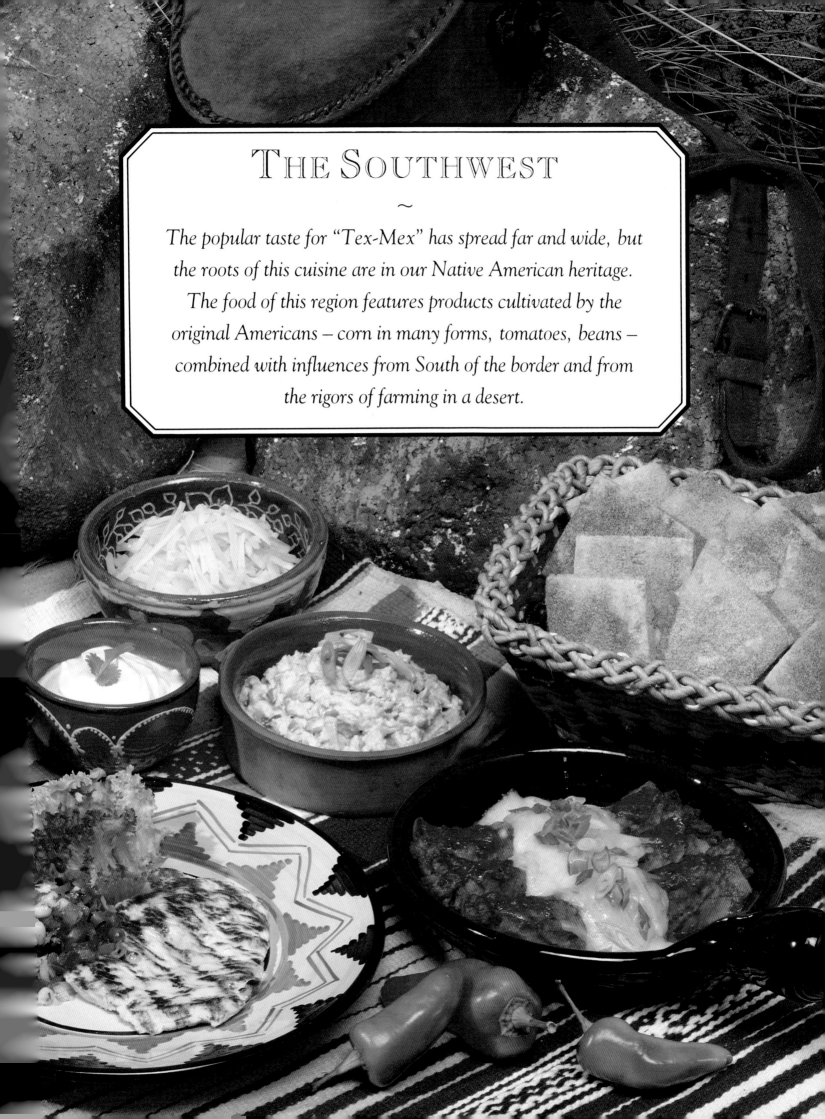

THE SOUTHWEST

~

The popular taste for "Tex-Mex" has spread far and wide, but the roots of this cuisine are in our Native American heritage. The food of this region features products cultivated by the original Americans – corn in many forms, tomatoes, beans – combined with influences from South of the border and from the rigors of farming in a desert.

Tortilla Soup

SERVES 4–6

1 tablespoon vegetable oil

1 onion, minced

1 large garlic clove, minced

2 medium tomatoes, peeled, seeded, and chopped

½ teaspoon salt

2 quarts chicken stock

1 carrot, diced

1 small zucchini, diced

1 skinless boneless chicken breast half, cooked and shredded

¼ cup canned green chilies, chopped

FOR GARNISHING

4 corn tortillas

oil for frying

1 small ripe avocado

2 scallions, chopped

chopped fresh coriander (cilantro)

shredded Monterey Jack cheese (optional)

1 ▲ Heat the oil in a saucepan. Add the onion and garlic and cook over medium heat until just softened, 5–8 minutes. Add the tomatoes and salt and cook 5 minutes more.

2 Stir in the stock. Bring to a boil, then lower the heat and simmer, covered, about 15 minutes.

3 ▲ Meanwhile, for the garnish, trim the tortillas into squares, then cut them into strips.

4 ▲ Put a ½-inch layer of oil in a skillet and heat until hot but not smoking. Add the tortilla strips, in batches, and fry until just beginning to brown, turning occasionally. Remove with a slotted spoon and drain on paper towels.

5 Add the carrot to the soup. Cook, covered, 10 minutes. Add the zucchini, chicken, and chilies and continue cooking, uncovered, until the vegetables are just tender, about 5 minutes more.

6 Meanwhile, peel and pit the avocado. Chop into a fine dice.

7 Divide the tortilla strips among 4 soup bowls. Sprinkle with the avocado. Ladle in the soup, then scatter scallions and coriander on top. Serve immediately, with shredded Monterey Jack cheese if desired.

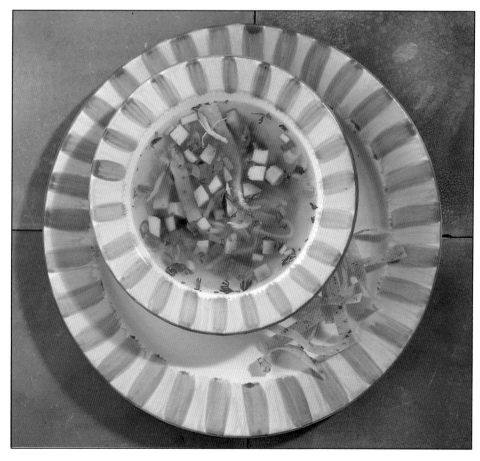

Spicy Bean Soup

SERVES 6–8

1 cup dried black beans, soaked overnight and drained

1 cup dried kidney beans, soaked overnight and drained

2 bay leaves

6 tablespoons coarse salt

2 tablespoons olive or vegetable oil

3 carrots, chopped

1 onion, chopped

1 celery stalk

1 garlic clove, minced

1 teaspoon ground cumin

¼–½ teaspoon cayenne

½ teaspoon dried oregano

salt and pepper

⅓ cup red wine

1 quart beef stock

1 cup water

FOR GARNISHING

sour cream

chopped fresh coriander (cilantro)

3 Heat the oil in a large flameproof casserole. Add the carrots, onion, celery, and garlic and cook over low heat, stirring, until softened, 8–10 minutes. Stir in the cumin, cayenne, oregano, and salt to taste.

4 ▼ Add the wine, stock, and water and stir to mix. Add the beans. Bring to a boil, reduce the heat, then cover and simmer about 20 minutes, stirring occasionally.

5 ▲ Transfer half of the soup (including most of the solids) to a food processor or blender. Process until smooth. Return to the pan and stir to combine well.

6 Reheat the soup if necessary and taste for seasoning. Serve hot, garnished with sour cream and chopped fresh coriander.

1 ▲ Put the black beans and kidney beans in two separate pots. To each, add fresh cold water to cover and a bay leaf. Bring to a boil, then cover, and simmer 30 minutes.

2 Add 3 tablespoons coarse salt to each pot and continue simmering until the beans are tender, about 30 minutes more. Drain and let cool slightly. Discard the bay leaves.

Desert Nachos

SERVES 2

1 6-ounce bag blue corn tortilla chips or
ordinary tortilla chips

2–4 tablespoons chopped pickled
jalapeños, according to taste

⅓ cup sliced black olives

2 cups shredded Monterey Jack cheese

FOR SERVING

guacamole

tomato salsa

sour cream

1 Preheat the oven to 350°F.

2 ▲ Put the tortilla chips in a 13- ×
9-inch baking dish and spread them
out evenly. Sprinkle the jalapeños,
olives, and cheese evenly over the
tortilla chips.

3 ▼ Place in the top of the oven and
bake until the cheese melts, 10–15
minutes. Serve the nachos at once,
with the guacamole, tomato salsa,
and sour cream for dipping.

Huevos Rancheros

SERVES 4

1 17-ounce can refried beans

1¼ cups enchilada sauce

oil for frying

4 corn tortillas

4 eggs

salt and pepper

1¼ cups shredded Monterey Jack or
cheddar cheese

1 ▼ Heat the beans in a saucepan.
Cover and set aside.

2 Heat the enchilada sauce in a small
saucepan. Cover and set aside.

3 Preheat the oven to 160°F.

4 ▲ Put a ¼-inch layer of oil in a
small nonstick skillet and heat. When
hot, add the tortillas, one at a time,
and fry until just crisp, about 30
seconds per side. Drain the tortillas on
paper towels and keep them warm on
a baking sheet in the oven. Discard
the oil used for frying.

5 Let the skillet cool slightly, then
wipe it with a paper towel to remove
all but a film of oil. Heat the skillet
over low heat. Break in 2 eggs and
cook until the whites are just set.
Season with salt and pepper, then
transfer to the oven to keep warm.
Repeat to cook the remaining eggs.

6 ▼ To serve, place a tortilla on
each of 4 plates. Spread a layer of
refried beans over each tortilla, then
top each with an egg. Spoon over the
warm enchilada sauce, then sprinkle
with the cheese. Serve hot.

Desert Nachos (top), Huevos Rancheros

Arizona Jalapeño-Onion Quiche

SERVES 6

1 tablespoon butter

2 onions, sliced

4 scallions, cut in ½-inch pieces

½ teaspoon ground cumin

1–2 tablespoons chopped canned
    jalapeños

4 eggs

1¼ cups milk

½ teaspoon salt

⅔ cup shredded Monterey Jack or
    cheddar cheese

FOR THE CRUST

1½ cups flour

¼ teaspoon salt

¼ teaspoon cayenne

6 tablespoons cold butter

6 tablespoons cold margarine

2–4 tablespoons ice water

1 For the crust, sift the flour, salt, and cayenne into a bowl. Using a pastry blender or 2 knives, cut in the butter and margarine until the mixture resembles coarse meal. Sprinkle with 2 tablespoons ice water and mix until the dough holds together. If the dough is too crumbly, add a little more water, 1 tablespoon at a time. Gather the dough into a ball and flatten into a disk. Wrap the dough in wax paper and refrigerate at least 30 minutes.

2 Preheat the oven to 375°F.

3 Roll out the dough to a thickness of about ⅛ inch. Use to line a 9-inch fluted tart pan that has a removable base. Prick the bottom of the quiche shell all over with a fork. Line the shell with wax paper and fill with dried beans.

4 Bake until the pastry has just set, 12–15 minutes. Remove from the oven and carefully lift out the paper and beans. Prick the bottom of the pastry shell all over. Return to the oven and bake until golden, 5–8 minutes more. Leave the oven on.

5 ▲ Melt the butter in a nonstick skillet. Add the onions and cook over medium heat until softened, about 5 minutes. Add the scallions and cook 1 minute more. Stir in the cumin and jalapeños and set aside.

6 In a mixing bowl, combine the eggs, milk, and salt and whisk until thoroughly blended.

7 ▲ Spoon the onion mixture into the pastry shell. Sprinkle with the cheese, then pour in the egg mixture.

8 Bake until the filling is golden and set, 30–40 minutes. Serve hot or at room temperature.

San Antonio Tortilla

SERVES 4

1 tablespoon vegetable oil

½ onion, sliced

1 small green bell pepper, seeded and sliced

1 garlic clove, minced

1 tomato, chopped

6 black olives, chopped

3 small potatoes (about 10 ounces total), cooked and sliced

2 ounces sliced chorizo, cut in strips

1 tablespoon chopped canned jalapeños, or to taste

½ cup shredded cheddar cheese

6 extra large eggs

3 tablespoons milk

½–¾ teaspoon salt

¼ teaspoon ground cumin

¼ teaspoon dried oregano

¼ teaspoon paprika

black pepper

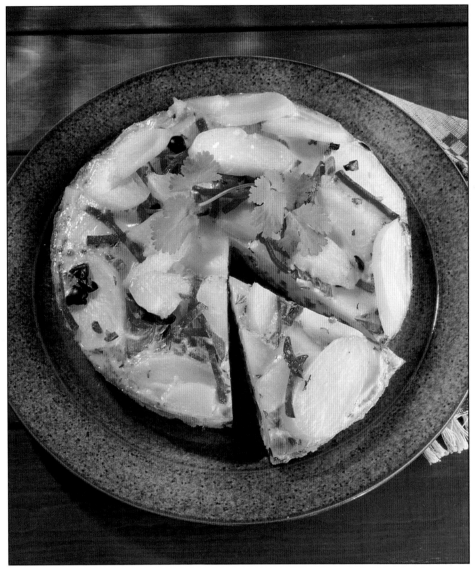

1 Preheat the oven to 375°F.

2 ▲ Heat the oil in a nonstick skillet. Add the onion, bell pepper, and garlic and cook over medium heat until softened, 5–8 minutes.

3 Transfer the vegetables to a 9-inch round nonstick cake pan. Add the tomato, olives, potatoes, chorizo, and jalapeños. Sprinkle with the cheese and set aside.

4 ▲ In a bowl, combine the eggs and milk and whisk until frothy. Add the salt, cumin, oregano, paprika, and pepper to taste. Whisk to blend.

5 Pour the egg mixture into the vegetable mixture, tilting the pan to spread it evenly.

6 ▲ Bake until set and lightly golden, about 30 minutes. Serve hot or cold.

Santa Fe Shrimp Salad

SERVES 4

1 pound cooked peeled shrimp

2 scallions, chopped

2 tablespoons fresh lemon juice

2 tablespoons extra-virgin olive oil

1 teaspoon salt

6 cups shredded lettuce

1 large ripe avocado

1 cup tomato salsa

FOR GARNISHING

fresh coriander (cilantro) sprigs

lime slices

1 ▲ In a bowl, combine the shrimp, scallions, lemon juice, oil, and salt. Mix well and set aside.

2 ▲ Line 4 plates (or a large platter) with the shredded lettuce.

3 ▲ Halve the avocado and remove the pit. With a small melon baller, scoop out balls of avocado and add to the shrimp mixture. Scrape the remaining avocado flesh into the salsa and stir. Add the salsa to the shrimp mixture and stir gently to blend.

4 ▲ Divide the shrimp mixture among the plates, piling it in the center. Garnish each salad with fresh coriander sprigs and slices of lime, and serve immediately.

Pinto Bean Salad

SERVES 4

1½ cups dried pinto beans, soaked
    overnight and drained

1 bay leaf

3 tablespoons coarse salt

2 ripe tomatoes, diced

4 scallions, minced

FOR THE DRESSING

¼ cup fresh lemon juice

salt and pepper

6 tablespoons olive oil

1 garlic clove, minced

3 tablespoons chopped fresh coriander
    (cilantro)

1 ▲ Put the beans in a large pot.
Add fresh cold water to cover and the
bay leaf. Bring to a boil, then cover,
and simmer 30 minutes. Add the salt
and continue simmering until tender,
about 30 minutes more. Drain and let
cool slightly. Discard the bay leaf.

2 ▲ For the dressing, mix the lemon
juice and 1 teaspoon salt with a fork
until dissolved. Gradually stir in the
oil until thick. Add the garlic,
coriander, and pepper to taste.

3 ▲ While the beans are still warm,
place them in a large bowl. Add the
dressing and toss to coat. Let the
beans cool completely.

4 ▼ Add the tomatoes and scallions
and toss to coat evenly. Let stand at
least 30 minutes before serving.

Chiles Rellenos

SERVES 4

8 large green bell peppers or fresh green chilies such as poblano

1–2 tablespoons vegetable oil, plus more for frying

4 cups shredded Monterey Jack cheese

4 eggs, separated

2/3 cup flour

FOR THE SAUCE

1 tablespoon vegetable oil

1 small onion, minced

1/4 teaspoon salt

1–2 teaspoons red pepper flakes

1/2 teaspoon ground cumin

1 cup beef or chicken stock

3 cups canned peeled tomatoes

1 ▲ For the sauce, heat the oil in a skillet. Add the onion and cook over low heat until just soft, about 8 minutes. Stir in the salt, pepper flakes, cumin, stock, and tomatoes. Cover and simmer gently 5 minutes, stirring occasionally.

2 Transfer to a food processor or blender and process until smooth. Strain into a clean pan. Taste for seasoning, and set aside.

~ COOK'S TIP ~

If necessary, work in batches, but do not coat the peppers until you are ready to fry them.

3 Preheat the broiler.

4 ▲ Brush the bell peppers or chilies lightly all over with oil. Lay them on a baking sheet. Broil as close to the heat as possible until blackened all over, 5–8 minutes. Cover with a clean dishtowel and set aside.

5 ▲ When cool enough to handle, remove the charred skin. Carefully slit the peppers or chilies and scoop out the seeds. If using chilies, wear rubber gloves. For less chili-heat, gently remove the white veins.

6 ▲ With your hands, form the cheese into 8 cylinders that are slightly shorter than the peppers. Place the cheese cylinders inside the peppers. Secure the slits with wooden toothpicks. Set aside.

7 ▲ Beat the egg whites until just stiff. Add the egg yolks, one at a time, beating on low speed just to incorporate them. Beat in 1 tablespoon of the flour.

8 Put a 1-inch layer of oil in a skillet or frying pan. Heat until hot but not smoking (to test, drop a scrap of batter in the oil: if the oil sizzles, it is hot enough for frying).

9 ▲ Coat the peppers lightly in flour all over; shake off any excess. Dip into the egg batter, then place in the hot oil. Fry until brown on one side, about 2 minutes. Turn carefully and brown the other side.

10 Reheat the sauce and serve with the chiles rellenos.

~ VARIATION ~

If using bell peppers instead of green chillies, mix the grated cheese with 1/2–1 tablespoon hot chili powder for a more authentic Southwest taste.

Black Bean Burritos

SERVES 4

1 cup dried black beans, soaked overnight and drained

1 bay leaf

3 tablespoons coarse salt

1 small red onion, minced

2 cups shredded Monterey Jack cheese

1–3 tablespoons chopped pickled jalapeños

1 tablespoon chopped fresh coriander (cilantro)

3½ cups tomato salsa

8 flour tortillas

diced avocado, for serving

1 ▲ Place the beans in a large pot. Add fresh cold water to cover and the bay leaf. Bring to a boil, then cover, and simmer 30 minutes. Add the salt and continue simmering until tender, about 30 minutes more. Drain and let cool slightly. Discard the bay leaf.

2 Preheat the oven to 350°F. Grease a rectangular baking dish.

3 ▲ In a bowl, combine the beans, onion, half the cheese, the jalapeños, coriander, and 1 cup of the salsa. Stir to blend and taste for seasoning.

4 ▲ Place 1 tortilla on a work surface. Spread a large spoonful of the filling down the middle, then roll up to enclose the filling. Place the burrito in the prepared dish, seam side down. Repeat with the remaining tortillas.

5 ▲ Sprinkle the remaining cheese over the burritos, in a line down the middle. Bake until the cheese melts, about 15 minutes.

6 Serve the burritos immediately, with avocado and the remaining salsa.

Black Bean Chili

Serves 6

2 cups dried black beans, soaked overnight and drained

2 tablespoons coarse salt

2 tablespoons vegetable oil

2 onions, chopped

1 green bell pepper, seeded and chopped

4 garlic cloves, minced

2 pounds ground chuck

1½ tablespoons ground cumin

½ teaspoon cayenne, or to taste

2½ teaspoons paprika

2 tablespoons dried oregano

1 teaspoon salt

3 tablespoons tomato paste

3 cups chopped peeled fresh or canned tomatoes

½ cup red wine

1 bay leaf

For serving

chopped fresh coriander (cilantro)

sour cream

shredded Monterey Jack or cheddar cheese

1 Put the beans in a large pot. Add fresh cold water to cover. Bring to a boil, then cover and simmer 30 minutes. Add the coarse salt and continue simmering until the beans are tender, about 30 minutes or longer. Drain and set aside.

2 Heat the oil in a large saucepan or flameproof casserole. Add the onions and bell pepper. Cook the vegetables over medium heat until just softened, about 5 minutes, stirring occasionally. Stir in the garlic and continue cooking 1 minute more.

3 Add the beef and cook over high heat, stirring frequently, until browned and crumbly. Reduce the heat and stir in the cumin, cayenne, paprika, oregano, and salt.

4 ▼ Add the tomato paste, tomatoes, drained black beans, wine, and bay leaf and stir well. Simmer 20 minutes, stirring occasionally.

5 ▲ Taste for seasoning. Remove the bay leaf and serve immediately, with chopped fresh coriander, sour cream, and shredded cheese.

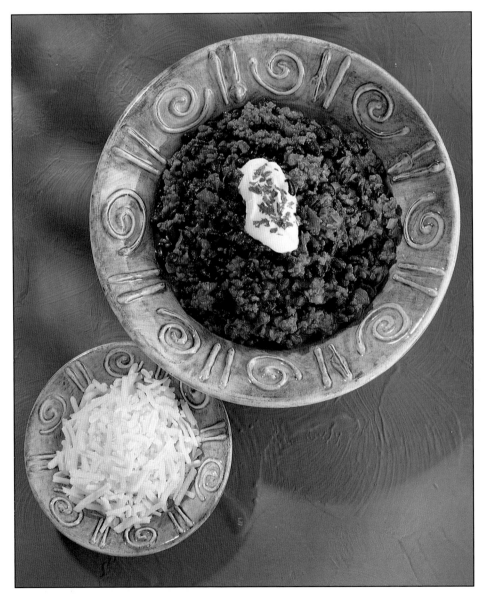

Red Snapper with Cilantro Salsa

SERVES 4

4 red snapper fillets, about 6 ounces each

salt and pepper

1½ tablespoons vegetable oil

1 tablespoon butter

FOR THE SALSA

2 cups fresh coriander (cilantro) leaves

1 cup olive oil

2 garlic cloves, chopped

2 tomatoes, cored and chopped

2 tablespoons fresh orange juice

1 tablespoon sherry vinegar

1 teaspoon salt

1 ▲ For the salsa, place the coriander, oil, and garlic in a food processor or blender. Process until almost smooth. Add the tomatoes and pulse on and off several times; the mixture should be slightly chunky.

2 ▲ Transfer to a bowl. Stir in the orange juice, vinegar, and salt. Set the salsa aside.

3 ▲ Rinse the fish fillets and pat dry. Sprinkle on both sides with salt and pepper. Heat the oil and butter in a large nonstick skillet. When hot, add the fish and cook until opaque throughout, 2–3 minutes on each side. Work in batches, if necessary.

4 ▲ Carefully transfer the fillets to warmed dinner plates. Top each with a spoonful of salsa. Serve additional salsa on the side.

Cornmeal-Coated Gulf Shrimp

SERVES 4

¾ cup cornmeal

1–2 teaspoons cayenne

½ teaspoon ground cumin

1 teaspoon salt

2 tablespoons chopped fresh coriander (cilantro) or parsley

2 pounds large raw Gulf shrimp, peeled and deveined

flour, for dredging

¼ cup vegetable oil

1 cup shredded Monterey Jack or cheddar cheese

FOR SERVING

lime wedges

tomato salsa

1 Preheat the broiler.

2 ▲ In a bowl, combine the cornmeal, cayenne, cumin, salt, and coriander or parsley.

3 ▲ Coat the shrimp lightly in flour, then dip in water and roll in the cornmeal mixture to coat.

4 ▼ Heat the oil in a nonstick skillet. When hot, add the shrimp, in batches if necessary. Cook until they are opaque throughout, 2–3 minutes on each side. Drain on paper towels.

5 ▲ Place the shrimp in a large baking dish, or individual dishes. Sprinkle the cheese evenly over the top. Broil about 3 inches from the heat until the cheese melts, 2–3 minutes. Serve immediately, with lime wedges and salsa.

Galveston Chicken

SERVES 4

3½-pound chicken

juice of 1 lemon

4 garlic cloves, minced

1 tablespoon cayenne

1 tablespoon paprika

1 tablespoon dried oregano

½ teaspoon coarse black pepper

2 teaspoons olive oil

1 teaspoon salt

~ COOK'S TIP ~

Roasting chicken in an oven that has not been preheated produces a particularly crispy skin.

1 ▼ With a sharp knife or poultry shears, remove the backbone from the chicken. Turn it breast side up. With the heel of your hand, press down to break the breastbone, and open the chicken flat like a book. Insert a skewer through the chicken, at the thighs, to keep it flat during cooking.

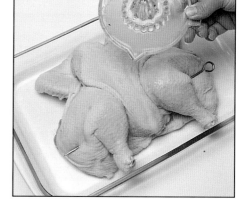

2 ▲ Place the chicken in a shallow dish and pour over the lemon juice.

3 ▲ In a small bowl, combine the garlic, cayenne, paprika, oregano, pepper, and oil. Mix well. Rub evenly over the surface of the chicken.

4 Cover and let marinate 2–3 hours at room temperature, or refrigerate overnight (return to room temperature before roasting).

5 Season the chicken with salt on both sides. Transfer it to a shallow roasting pan.

6 Put the pan in a cold oven and set the temperature to 400°F. Roast until the chicken is done, about 1 hour, turning occasionally and basting with the pan juices. To test for doneness, prick with a skewer: the juices that run out should be clear.

Turkey Breasts with Tomato-Corn Salsa

SERVES 4

4 skinless boneless turkey breast halves, about 6 ounces each

2 tablespoons fresh lemon juice

2 tablespoons olive oil

½ teaspoon ground cumin

½ teaspoon dried oregano

1 teaspoon coarse black pepper

salt

FOR THE SALSA

1 fresh hot green chili pepper

1 pound tomatoes, seeded and chopped

1½ cups corn kernels, freshly cooked or thawed frozen

3 scallions, chopped

1 tablespoon chopped fresh parsley

2 tablespoons chopped fresh coriander (cilantro)

2 tablespoons fresh lemon juice

3 tablespoons olive oil

1 teaspoon salt

1 ▲ With a meat mallet, pound the turkey breasts between 2 sheets of wax paper until thin.

~ **VARIATION** ~

Use the cooked turkey, thinly sliced and combined with the salsa, as a filling for warmed flour tortillas.

2 ▲ In a shallow dish, combine the lemon juice, oil, cumin, oregano, and pepper. Add the turkey and turn to coat. Cover and let stand at least 2 hours, or refrigerate overnight.

3 For the salsa, roast the chili over a gas flame, holding it with tongs, until charred on all sides. (Alternatively, char the skin under the broiler.) Let cool 5 minutes. Wearing rubber gloves, carefully rub off the charred skin. For a less hot flavor, discard the seeds. Chop the chili finely and place in a bowl.

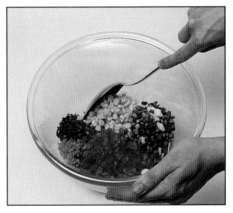

4 ▲ Add the remaining salsa ingredients to the chili and toss well to blend. Set aside.

5 Remove the turkey from the marinade. Season lightly on both sides with salt to taste.

6 Heat a ridged grill pan. When hot, add the turkey breasts and cook until browned, about 3 minutes. Turn and cook the meat on the other side until it is cooked through, 3–4 minutes more. Serve the turkey immediately, accompanied by salsa.

Spicy New Mexico Pork Stew

SERVES 6

1 cup water

1 tablespoon tomato paste

4 garlic cloves, minced

2 teaspoons dried oregano

2½ teaspoons ground cumin

2 teaspoons salt

1–3 tablespoons red pepper flakes

4 pounds boneless pork shoulder, cubed

2 onions, thickly sliced

warm flour tortillas, for serving

1 In a large casserole, combine the water, tomato paste, garlic, oregano, cumin, and salt. Add red pepper flakes to taste and stir to mix.

2 ▲ Add the pork cubes and toss to coat them evenly. Cover and allow to marinate 6–8 hours, or overnight, in the refrigerator.

3 Preheat the oven to 300°F.

4 ▼ Cover the casserole and put it in the oven. Cook for 1½ hours. Add the onions and cook 1½ hours more. Serve with flour tortillas.

Turkey-Chorizo Tacos

SERVES 4

1 tablespoon vegetable oil

1 pound ground turkey

1 teaspoon salt

1 teaspoon ground cumin

12 taco shells

3 ounces chorizo, minced

3 scallions, chopped

2 tomatoes, chopped

2½ cups shredded lettuce

2 cups shredded Monterey Jack cheese

FOR SERVING

tomato salsa

guacamole

~ **VARIATION** ~

For Chicken Tacos, use minced chicken instead of the turkey.

1 Preheat the oven to 350°F.

2 ▲ Heat the oil in a nonstick skillet. Add the turkey, salt, and cumin and sauté over medium heat until the turkey is cooked through, 5–8 minutes. Stir frequently to prevent large lumps from forming.

3 Meanwhile, arrange the taco shells in one layer on a large baking sheet and heat in the oven about 10 minutes, or according to the directions on the package.

4 Add the chorizo and scallions to the turkey and stir to mix. Cook until just warmed through, stirring the mixture occasionally.

5 ▲ To assemble each taco, place 1–2 spoonfuls of the turkey mixture in the bottom of a warmed taco shell. Top with a generous sprinkling of chopped tomato, shredded lettuce, and shredded cheese.

6 Serve immediately, with tomato salsa and guacamole.

Spicy New Mexico Pork Stew (top), Turkey-Chorizo Tacos

Pork Chops with Sour Green Chili Salsa

SERVES 4

2 tablespoons vegetable oil

1 tablespoon fresh lemon juice

2 teaspoons ground cumin

1 teaspoon dried oregano

salt and pepper

8 pork loin chops, about ¾ inch thick

FOR THE SALSA

2 fresh hot green chili peppers

2 green bell peppers, seeded and chopped

1 tomato, peeled and seeded

½ onion, coarsely chopped

4 scallions

1 pickled jalapeño, stem removed

2 tablespoons olive oil

2 tablespoons fresh lime juice

3 tablespoons cider vinegar

1 teaspoon salt

1 In a small bowl, combine the vegetable oil, lemon juice, cumin, and oregano. Add pepper to taste and stir to blend.

2 ▼ Arrange the pork chops in one layer in a shallow dish. Brush each with the oil mixture on both sides. Cover and let stand 2–3 hours, or refrigerate overnight.

3 ▲ For the salsa, roast the chilies over a gas flame, holding them with tongs, until charred on all sides. (Alternatively, char the skins under the broiler.) Let cool 5 minutes. Wearing rubber gloves, remove the charred skin. For a less hot flavor, discard the seeds.

4 Place the chilies in a food processor or blender. Add the remaining salsa ingredients. Process until finely chopped; do not purée.

5 Transfer the salsa to a heavy saucepan and simmer 15 minutes, stirring occasionally. Set aside.

6 ▲ Season the pork chops. Heat a ridged grill pan. (Alternatively, preheat the broiler.) When hot, add the pork chops and cook until browned, about 5 minutes. Turn and continue cooking until done, 5–7 minutes more. Work in batches, if necessary.

7 Serve immediately, with the sour green chili salsa.

Pork Fajitas

SERVES 6

juice of 3 limes

6 tablespoons olive oil

1 teaspoon dried oregano

1 teaspoon ground cumin

½ teaspoon red pepper flakes

1½ pounds pork tenderloin, cut across
    in 3-inch pieces

salt and pepper

2 large onions, halved and thinly sliced

1 large green bell pepper, seeded and
    thinly sliced lengthwise

FOR SERVING

12–15 flour tortillas, warmed

tomato salsa

guacamole

sour cream

1 ▲ In a shallow dish, combine the lime juice, 3 tablespoons of the oil, the oregano, cumin, and red pepper flakes and mix well. Add the pork pieces and turn to coat. Cover and let stand 1 hour, or refrigerate overnight.

2 Remove the pieces of pork from the marinade. Pat them dry and season with salt and pepper.

3 Heat a ridged grill pan. When hot, add the pork and cook over high heat, turning occasionally, until browned on all sides and cooked through, about 10–12 minutes.

4 ▼ Meanwhile, heat the remaining oil in a large skillet. Add the onions and bell pepper. Stir in ½ teaspoon salt and cook until the vegetables are very soft, about 15 minutes. Stir occasionally. Remove from the heat and set aside.

5 ▲ Slice the pork pieces into thin strips. Add to the onion mixture and reheat briefly if necessary.

6 Spoon a little of the pork mixture onto each tortilla. Garnish with salsa, guacamole, and sour cream, and roll up. Alternatively, the fajitas may be assembled at the table.

Lamb Stew with Cornmeal Dumplings

SERVES 6

1 tablespoon vegetable oil

1 large onion, chopped

1 large celery stalk, chopped

1 red bell pepper, seeded and chopped

1½ pounds boneless lamb, cubed

1 teaspoon salt, or to taste

3 medium tomatoes, cored and chopped

1 teaspoon ground cumin

⅛ teaspoon ground cinnamon

¼ teaspoon cayenne, or to taste

5 cups beef stock

2 zucchini (about ½ pound), quartered and chopped

FOR THE DUMPLINGS

1 cup cornmeal

2 tablespoons flour

2 teaspoons baking powder

½ teaspoon salt

1 extra large egg, beaten

2 tablespoons butter, melted

⅓ cup milk

1 Heat the oil in a large flameproof casserole. Add the onion and celery and cook over medium heat until just soft, about 5 minutes.

2 ▲ Add the bell pepper, lamb, and salt. Cook until the cubes of lamb are browned, 5–7 minutes more. Stir to brown them evenly.

3 Stir in the tomatoes, spices, and stock. Bring to a boil, skimming off any foam that rises to the surface. Reduce the heat, cover, and simmer gently 25 minutes. From time to time, skim off any surface fat.

4 Meanwhile, for the dumplings, heat about 2 inches of water in the bottom of a steamer.

5 ▲ Combine the cornmeal, flour, baking powder, and salt in a bowl. Make a well in the center and add the egg, butter, and milk. Stir with a fork until blended.

6 With your hands, shape the mixture into 6 balls, each about 2 inches in diameter.

7 ▲ When the water in the steamer is hot, place the dumplings in the steamer basket. Cover and steam about 20 minutes. (If necessary, add boiling water to replenish the bottom of the steamer.)

8 About 5 minutes before the stew has finished cooking, add the zucchini and stir to mix.

9 Ladle the stew into shallow bowls. Place a dumpling in the center of each and serve immediately.

Tamale Pie

SERVES 8

4 ounces bacon, chopped

1 onion, minced

1 pound lean ground beef

2–3 teaspoons chili powder

1 teaspoon salt

2 cups peeled fresh or canned
    tomatoes

⅓ cup chopped black olives

1 cup corn kernels, freshly cooked or
    thawed frozen

½ cup sour cream

1 cup shredded Monterey Jack cheese

FOR THE TAMALE CRUST

1–1¼ cups chicken stock

salt and pepper

1½ cups masa harina or cornmeal

6 tablespoons margarine or shortening

½ teaspoon baking powder

¼ cup milk

1 Preheat the oven to 375°F.

2 Cook the bacon in a large skillet until the fat is rendered, 2–3 minutes. Pour off excess fat, leaving 1–2 tablespoons. Add the onion and cook until just softened, about 5 minutes.

3 ▲ Add the beef, chili powder, and salt and cook 5 minutes, stirring to break up the meat. Stir in the tomatoes and cook 5 minutes more, breaking them up with a spoon.

4 ▲ Add the olives, corn, and sour cream, and mix well. Transfer to a 15-inch-long rectangular or oval baking dish. Set aside.

5 For the crust, bring the stock to a boil in a saucepan; season it with salt and pepper if necessary.

6 In a food processor, combine the masa harina or cornmeal, margarine or shortening, baking powder, and milk. Process until combined. With the machine on, gradually pour in the hot stock until a smooth, thick batter is obtained. If the batter is too thick to spread, add additional hot stock or water, a little at a time.

7 Pour the batter over the top of the beef mixture, spreading it evenly with a metal spatula.

8 Bake until the top is just browned, about 20 minutes. Sprinkle the surface evenly with the shredded cheese and continue baking until melted and bubbling, 10–15 minutes more. Serve immediately.

Beef Enchiladas

SERVES 4

2 pounds chuck steak
1 tablespoon vegetable oil, plus more for frying
1 teaspoon salt
1 teaspoon dried oregano
½ teaspoon ground cumin
1 onion, quartered
2 garlic cloves, crushed
4 cups enchilada sauce
12 corn tortillas
1 cup shredded Monterey Jack cheese
chopped scallions, for serving
sour cream, for serving

1 Preheat the oven to 325°F.

2 ▲ Place the meat on a sheet of foil. Rub all over with the oil. Sprinkle both sides with the salt, oregano, and cumin and rub in well. Add the onion and garlic. Top with another sheet of foil and roll up to seal the edges, leaving room for some steam expansion during cooking.

~ COOK'S TIP ~

Allow extra tortillas because some will break when dipping in the oil or sauce.

3 ▲ Place in a baking dish. Bake until the meat is tender enough to shred, about 3 hours. Remove the meat from the foil and shred with a fork. (This can be prepared 1–2 days in advance.)

4 ▲ Add ½ cup of the enchilada sauce to the beef. Stir well. Spoon a thin layer of enchilada sauce on the bottom of a rectangular baking dish, or in 4 individual baking dishes.

5 ▲ Place the remaining enchilada sauce in a skillet and warm gently.

6 ▲ Put a ½-inch layer of vegetable oil in a second skillet and heat until hot but not smoking. With tongs, lower a tortilla into the oil; the temperature is correct if it just sizzles. Cook 2 seconds, then turn and cook the other side 2 seconds. Lift out, drain over the skillet, and then transfer to the skillet of sauce. Dip in the sauce just to coat both sides.

7 ▲ Transfer the softened tortilla immediately to a plate. Spread 2–3 spoonfuls of the beef mixture down the center of the tortilla. Roll up and place seam-side down in the prepared dish. Repeat the process for the remaining tortillas.

8 Spoon the remaining sauce from the skillet over the enchiladas, spreading it to the ends. Sprinkle the cheese down the center.

9 Bake until the cheese just melts, 10–15 minutes. Sprinkle with chopped scallions and serve at once, with sour cream on the side.

Lone Star Steak and Potato Dinner

SERVES 4

3 tablespoons olive oil

5 large garlic cloves, minced

1 teaspoon coarse black pepper

½ teaspoon ground allspice

1 teaspoon ground cumin

½ teaspoon chili powder

2 teaspoons dried oregano

1 tablespoon cider vinegar

4 boneless sirloin steaks, about ¾ inch thick

salt

tomato salsa, for serving

freshly cooked corn-on-the-cob, for serving (optional)

FOR THE POTATOES

¼ cup vegetable oil

1 onion, chopped

1 teaspoon salt

2 pounds potatoes, boiled and diced

2–5 tablespoons chopped canned green chilies, according to taste

1 ▲ Heat the olive oil in a heavy skillet. When hot, add the garlic and cook, stirring often, until tender and just brown, about 3 minutes; do not let the garlic burn.

2 Transfer the garlic and oil to a shallow dish large enough to hold the steaks in one layer.

3 ▲ Add the pepper, spices, herbs, and vinegar to the garlic and stir to blend thoroughly. If necessary, add just enough water to obtain a moderately thick paste.

4 ▲ Add the steaks to the dish and turn to coat evenly on both sides with the spice mixture. Cover and let stand 2 hours, or refrigerate the steaks overnight. (Bring them to room temperature before cooking.)

~ VARIATION ~

The steaks can also be cooked on a charcoal grill. Prepare the fire, and when the coals are glowing red and covered with grey ash, spread them in a single layer. Cook the steaks in the center of an oiled grill rack set about 5 inches above the coals for 1 minute per side to sear them. Move them away from the center and cook 10–12 minutes longer for medium rare, turning once.

---

5 ▲ For the potatoes, heat the oil in a large nonstick skillet. Add the onion and salt. Cook over medium heat until softened, about 5 minutes. Add the potatoes and chilies. Cook, stirring occasionally, until well browned, 15–20 minutes.

6 ▲ Season the steaks on both sides with salt to taste. Heat a ridged grill pan. When hot, add the steaks and cook, turning once, until done to your taste. Allow about 2 minutes on each side for medium-rare, and 3–4 minutes for well done.

7 ▲ If necessary, briefly reheat the potatoes. Serve immediately, with the tomato salsa and corn, if using.

Guacamole

MAKES 2 CUPS

3 large ripe avocados
3 scallions, minced
1 garlic clove, minced
1 tablespoon olive oil
1 tablespoon sour cream
½ teaspoon salt
2 tablespoons fresh lemon or lime juice

1 ▲ Halve the avocados and remove the pits. Peel the halves. Put the avocado flesh in a large bowl.

2 ▲ With a fork, mash the avocado flesh coarsely.

3 Add the scallions, garlic, olive oil, sour cream, salt, and lemon or lime juice. Mash until well blended, but do not overwork the mixture. Small chunks of avocado should still remain. Taste the guacamole and adjust the seasoning if necessary, with more salt or lemon or lime juice.

4 ▼ Transfer to a serving bowl. Serve immediately.

~ COOK'S TIP ~

Guacamole does not keep well, but, if necessary, it can be stored in the refrigerator a few hours. Cover the surface with plastic wrap to prevent discoloring.

Tomato Salsa

MAKES 3½ CUPS

1 fresh hot green chili pepper, seeded if desired, chopped
1 garlic clove
½ red onion, coarsely chopped
3 scallions, chopped
¼ cup fresh coriander (cilantro) leaves
1½ pounds ripe tomatoes, seeded and coarsely chopped
1–3 canned green chilies
1 tablespoon olive oil
2 tablespoons fresh lime or lemon juice
½ teaspoon salt, or to taste
2–3 tablespoons tomato juice or cold water

1 In a food processor or blender, combine the fresh green chili, garlic, red onion, scallions, and coriander. Process until finely chopped.

2 ▼ Add the tomatoes, canned chilies, olive oil, lime or lemon juice, salt, and tomato juice or water. Pulse on and off until just chopped; the salsa should be chunky.

3 ▲ Transfer to a bowl and taste for seasoning. Let stand at least 30 minutes before serving. This salsa is best served the day it is made.

~ COOK'S TIP ~

For less heat, remove the seeds from fresh and canned chilies.

Guacamole (top), Tomato Salsa

Tomato Rice

SERVES 4

2 cups unsalted chicken or beef stock

1½ tablespoons vegetable oil

1 small onion, minced

1 cup long-grain rice

1 teaspoon salt

½ teaspoon ground cumin

1 medium-size tomato, peeled, seeded, and chopped

1 tablespoon tomato paste

1 tablespoon chopped fresh coriander (cilantro)

1 Place the stock in a saucepan and heat until just simmering. Remove from the heat, cover, and set aside.

2 ▼ Heat the oil in a large heavy saucepan. Add the onion and rice and cook over medium heat until the onion is just softened, about 5 minutes. Stir in the salt, cumin, tomato, and tomato paste and cook 1 minute more, stirring.

3 ▲ Gradually add the warm stock, stirring to blend. Bring to a boil, then lower the heat, cover, and cook until the rice is tender and all the liquid is absorbed, 30–40 minutes.

4 Fluff the rice with a fork and stir in the coriander. Serve immediately.

Enchilada Sauce

MAKES ABOUT 6 CUPS

4 16-ounce cans peeled plum tomatoes, drained

3 garlic cloves, coarsely chopped

1 onion, coarsely chopped

2–4 tablespoons ground red chili

1 teaspoon cayenne, or to taste

1 teaspoon ground cumin

½ teaspoon dried oregano

½ teaspoon salt

~ COOK'S TIP ~

Ground red chili is not the same thing as chili powder. If ground red chili is unavailable, use hot red pepper flakes and strain the sauce before using.

1 ▼ In a food processor or blender, combine the tomatoes, garlic, and onion. Process until smooth.

2 Pour and scrape the mixture into a heavy saucepan.

3 ▲ Add the remaining ingredients and stir to blend. Bring to a boil, stirring occasionally. Boil 2–3 minutes. Reduce the heat, cover, and simmer 15 minutes.

4 Dilute with ½–1 cup water, as necessary, to obtain a pouring consistency. Taste for seasoning; if a hotter sauce is desired, add more cayenne, not ground chili.

Tomato Rice (top), Enchilada Sauce

Navajo Fry Bread

MAKES 8 BREAD ROUNDS

2 cups flour

2 teaspoons baking powder

½ teaspoon salt

1 cup lukewarm water

oil for frying

1 Sift the flour, baking powder, and salt into a bowl. Pour in the water and stir quickly with a fork until the dough gathers into a ball.

2 ▼ With floured hands, gently knead the dough by rolling it around the bowl. Do not overknead; the dough should be very soft.

3 ▲ Divide the dough into 8 pieces. With floured hands, pat each piece into a round about 5 inches in diameter. Place the rounds on a floured baking sheet.

4 Put a 1-inch layer of oil in a heavy skillet and heat until hot but not smoking. To test the temperature, drop in a small piece of dough; if it bubbles immediately, the oil is ready.

5 ▲ Add the dough rounds to the hot oil and press down with a slotted spoon to submerge them. Release the dough and cook until puffed and golden on both sides, 3–5 minutes total, turning for even browning. Fry in batches, if necessary.

6 Drain the bread on paper towels and serve immediately. Good as an accompaniment for chili or with shredded cheese and an assortment of southwestern salsas. (Fry bread will not keep.)

Bean Dip

MAKES 3 CUPS

1½ cups dried pinto beans, soaked overnight and drained
1 bay leaf
3 tablespoons coarse salt
1 tablespoon vegetable oil
1 small onion, sliced
1 garlic clove, minced
2–4 canned hot green chilies (optional)
⅓ cup sour cream, plus more for garnishing
½ teaspoon ground cumin
hot pepper sauce
1 tablespoon chopped fresh coriander (cilantro)
tortilla chips, for serving

1 ▲ Place the beans in a large pot. Add fresh cold water to cover and the bay leaf. Bring to a boil, then cover, and simmer 30 minutes.

2 Add the coarse salt and continue simmering until the beans are tender, about 30 minutes or more.

3 Drain the beans, reserving ½ cup of the cooking liquid. Let cool slightly. Discard the bay leaf.

4 Heat the oil in a nonstick skillet. Add the onion and garlic and cook over low heat until just softened, 8–10 minutes, stirring occasionally.

5 ▲ In a food processor or blender, combine the beans, onion mixture, chilies if using, and the reserved cooking liquid. Process until the mixture resembles a coarse purée.

6 ▼ Transfer to a bowl and stir in the sour cream, cumin, and hot pepper sauce to taste. Stir in the coriander, garnish with sour cream, and serve warm, with tortilla chips.

Chocolate Cinnamon Cake with Banana Sauce

SERVES 6

4 1-ounce squares semisweet chocolate, finely chopped

½ cup (1 stick) unsalted butter, at room temperature

1 tablespoon instant coffee powder

5 eggs, separated

1 cup granulated sugar

1 cup flour

2 teaspoons ground cinnamon

FOR THE SAUCE

4 ripe bananas

¼ cup light brown sugar, firmly packed

1 tablespoon fresh lemon juice

¾ cup whipping cream

1 tablespoon rum (optional)

1 Preheat the oven to 350°F. Grease an 8-inch round cake pan.

2 ▲ Combine the chocolate and butter in the top of a double boiler or in a heatproof bowl set over hot water. Stir until melted. Remove from the heat and stir in the coffee. Set aside.

3 Beat the egg yolks with the granulated sugar until thick and lemon-colored. Add the chocolate mixture and beat on low speed just to blend the mixtures evenly.

4 Sift together the flour and cinnamon into a bowl.

5 ▲ In another bowl, beat the egg whites until they hold stiff peaks.

6 ▲ Fold a dollop of whites into the chocolate mixture to lighten it. Fold in the remaining whites in 3 batches, alternating with the sifted flour.

7 ▲ Pour the batter into the prepared pan. Bake until a cake tester inserted in the center comes out clean, 40–50 minutes. Unmold the cake onto a wire rack.

8 Preheat the broiler.

9 ▲ For the sauce, slice the bananas into a shallow, heatproof dish. Add the brown sugar and lemon juice and stir to blend. Place under the broiler and cook, stirring occasionally, until the sugar is caramelized and bubbling, about 8 minutes.

10 ▲ Transfer the bananas to a bowl and mash with a fork until almost smooth. Stir in the cream and rum, if using. Serve the cake and sauce warm.

~ **VARIATION** ~

For a special occasion, top the cake slices with a scoop of ice cream (rum-raisin, chocolate, or vanilla) before adding the banana sauce. With this addition, the dessert will make at least 8 portions.

Mexican Hot Fudge Sundaes

SERVES 4

1 pint vanilla ice cream

1 pint coffee ice cream

2 large ripe bananas, sliced

whipped cream

toasted sliced almonds

FOR THE SAUCE

¼ cup light brown sugar, firmly packed

½ cup light corn syrup

3 tablespoons strong black coffee

1 teaspoon ground cinnamon

5 1-ounce squares bittersweet chocolate, broken up

⅓ cup whipping cream

3 tablespoons coffee liqueur (optional)

1 ▼ For the sauce, combine the brown sugar, corn syrup, coffee, and cinnamon in a heavy saucepan. Bring to a boil. Boil the mixture, stirring constantly, about 5 minutes.

2 ▲ Remove from the heat and stir in the chocolate. When melted and smooth, stir in the cream and liqueur, if using. Let the sauce cool just to lukewarm, or if made ahead, reheat gently while assembling the sundaes.

3 ▲ Fill sundae dishes with 1 scoop each of vanilla and coffee ice cream.

4 ▲ Arrange the bananas on the top of each dish. Pour the warm sauce over the bananas, then top each sundae with a generous rosette of whipped cream. Top with toasted almonds and serve immediately.

New Mexico Christmas Biscochitos

MAKES 24

1½ cups flour

1 teaspoon baking powder

⅛ teaspoon salt

½ cup (1 stick) unsalted butter, at room temperature

½ cup sugar

1 egg

1 teaspoon whole aniseed

1 tablespoon brandy

¼ cup sugar mixed with ½ teaspoon ground cinnamon, for sprinkling

1 Sift together the flour, baking powder, and salt. Set aside.

2 ▲ Beat the butter with the sugar until soft and fluffy. Add the egg, aniseed, and brandy and beat until incorporated. Fold in the dry ingredients just until blended to a dough. Refrigerate 30 minutes.

3 ▲ Preheat the oven to 350°F. Grease 2 cookie sheets.

4 On a lightly floured surface, roll out the chilled cookie dough to about ⅛-inch thickness.

5 ▲ With a cutter, pastry wheel, or knife, cut out the cookies into squares, diamonds, or other shapes. The traditional shape for biscochitos is a fleur-de-lis.

6 ▲ Place on the prepared cookie sheets and sprinkle lightly with the cinnamon sugar.

7 Bake until just barely golden, about 10 minutes. Cool on the sheet 5 minutes before transferring to a wire rack to cool completely. The cookies can be kept in an airtight container up to 1 week.

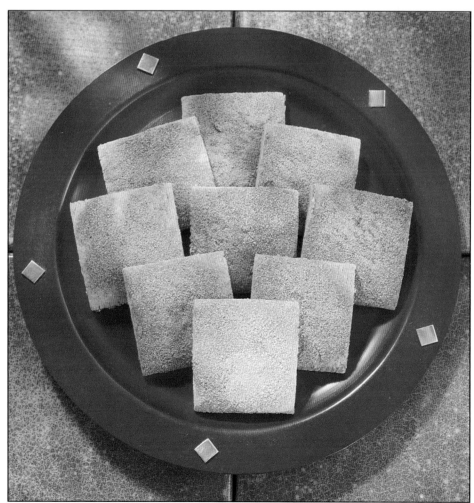

Pueblo Pastelitos

MAKES 16

2 cups dried fruit, such as apricots or prunes

½ cup light brown sugar, firmly packed

½ cup raisins

½ cup pine nuts or chopped almonds

½ teaspoon ground cinnamon

oil for frying

3 tablespoons granulated sugar mixed with 1 teaspoon ground cinnamon, for sprinkling

FOR THE PASTRY DOUGH

2 cups flour

¼ teaspoon baking powder

¼ teaspoon salt

2 teaspoons granulated sugar

4 tablespoons unsalted butter, chilled

2 tablespoons shortening

½–⅓ cup ice water

1 ▲ For the pastry dough, sift the flour, baking powder, salt, and sugar into a bowl. With a plastry blender or 2 knives, cut in the butter and shortening until the mixture resembles coarse meal. Sprinkle with ½ cup ice water and mix until the dough holds together. If the dough is too crumbly, add a little more water, 1 tablespoon at a time.

2 Gather the dough into a ball and flatten into a disk. Wrap the dough in wax paper and refrigerate it at least 30 minutes.

3 ▲ Place the dried fruit in a saucepan and add cold water to cover. Bring to a boil, then simmer gently until the fruit is soft enough to purée, about 30 minutes.

4 ▲ Drain the fruit and place in a food processor or blender. Process until smooth. Return the fruit purée to the saucepan. Add the brown sugar and cook, stirring constantly, until thick, about 5 minutes. Remove from the heat and stir in the raisins, pine nuts or almonds, and cinnamon. Allow the mixture to cool.

5 Roll out the chilled dough to about ⅛-inch thickness. Stamp out rounds with a 4-inch cookie cutter. (Roll and cut out in 2 batches if it is more convenient.)

~ COOK'S TIP ~

If desired, the pastry and the filling can both be made up to 2 days in advance and refrigerated.

6 ▲ Place a spoonful of the fruit filling in the center of each round.

7 ▲ Moisten the edge with a brush dipped in water, then fold over the dough to form a half-moon shape. With a fork, crimp the rounded edge.

8 ▲ Put a ½-inch layer of oil in a heavy skillet and heat until hot but not smoking (to test, drop a scrap of dough in the oil; if the oil sizzles, it is hot enough). Add the turnovers, a few at a time, and fry until golden on both sides, about 1½ minutes per side.

9 Drain briefly on paper towels, then sprinkle with the cinnamon sugar. Serve the pastelitos warm.

Flan

SERVES 8–10

3½ cups milk

½ cup whipping cream

1 cup sugar

1 cinnamon stick

8 extra large eggs

1 teaspoon vanilla extract

FOR THE CARAMEL

⅔ cup sugar

¼ cup water

1 In a saucepan, combine the milk, cream, sugar, and cinnamon. Scald over medium heat, stirring. Remove, cover, and let stand 30 minutes.

2 For the caramel, combine the sugar and water in a small, heavy saucepan over medium-high heat.

3 Bring to a boil, then simmer until the syrup begins to color; do not stir. When the syrup is a deep golden brown, dip the base of the pan in cold water to stop the cooking.

4 ▲ Quickly pour the caramel syrup into a 2½-quart mold and tilt the mold to coat the bottom evenly.

5 Preheat the oven to 350°F.

6 ▲ Reheat the milk mixture just to warm. Remove the cinnamon stick.

7 In a large bowl, combine the eggs and vanilla and mix together. Pour the milk mixture over the egg mixture, stirring constantly.

8 ▲ Place the caramel-coated mold in a large baking dish and add just enough hot water to come about 2 inches up the side of the mold. Pour the egg mixture through a strainer into the mold. Cover with foil.

9 Bake until the custard is just set, 40–50 minutes. Let cool in the water bath, then refrigerate at least 4 hours.

10 To unmold, run a knife around the inside of the mold. Place an inverted plate on top and flip over to release the flan. Scrape any remaining caramel onto the flan. Serve cold.

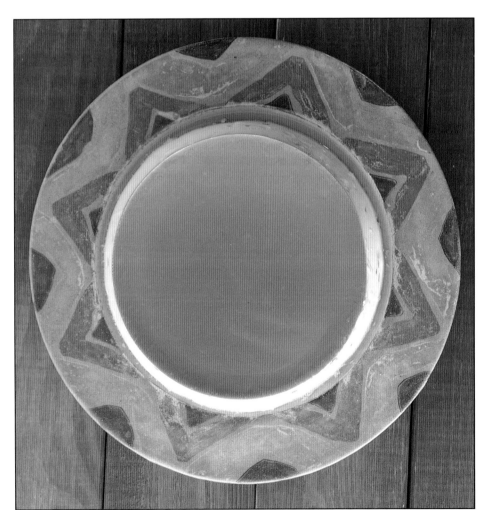

Southwestern Rice Pudding

SERVES 4–6

¼ cup raisins

2 cups water

1 cup short-grain rice

1 cinnamon stick

2 tablespoons sugar

2 cups milk

1 cup canned sweetened coconut cream

½ teaspoon vanilla extract

1 tablespoon butter

⅓ cup shredded coconut

ground cinnamon, for sprinkling

1 ▲ Put the raisins in a small bowl and add water to cover. Let soak.

2 ▲ In a medium-size saucepan, bring the water to a boil. Add the rice, cinnamon stick, and sugar and stir. Return to a boil, then lower the heat, cover, and simmer gently until the liquid is absorbed, 15–20 minutes.

3 ▼ Meanwhile, combine the milk, coconut cream, and vanilla in a bowl. Drain the raisins.

4 Remove the cinnamon stick from the pan. Add the milk mixture and drained raisins to the rice and stir to mix. Continue cooking, covered and stirring often, until the mixture is just thick, about 20 minutes. Do not overcook the rice.

5 Preheat the broiler.

6 Transfer the mixture to a heatproof serving dish. Dot with the butter and sprinkle coconut evenly over the surface. Broil about 5 inches from the heat until the top is just browned, 3–5 minutes. Sprinkle with cinnamon. Serve warm or cold.

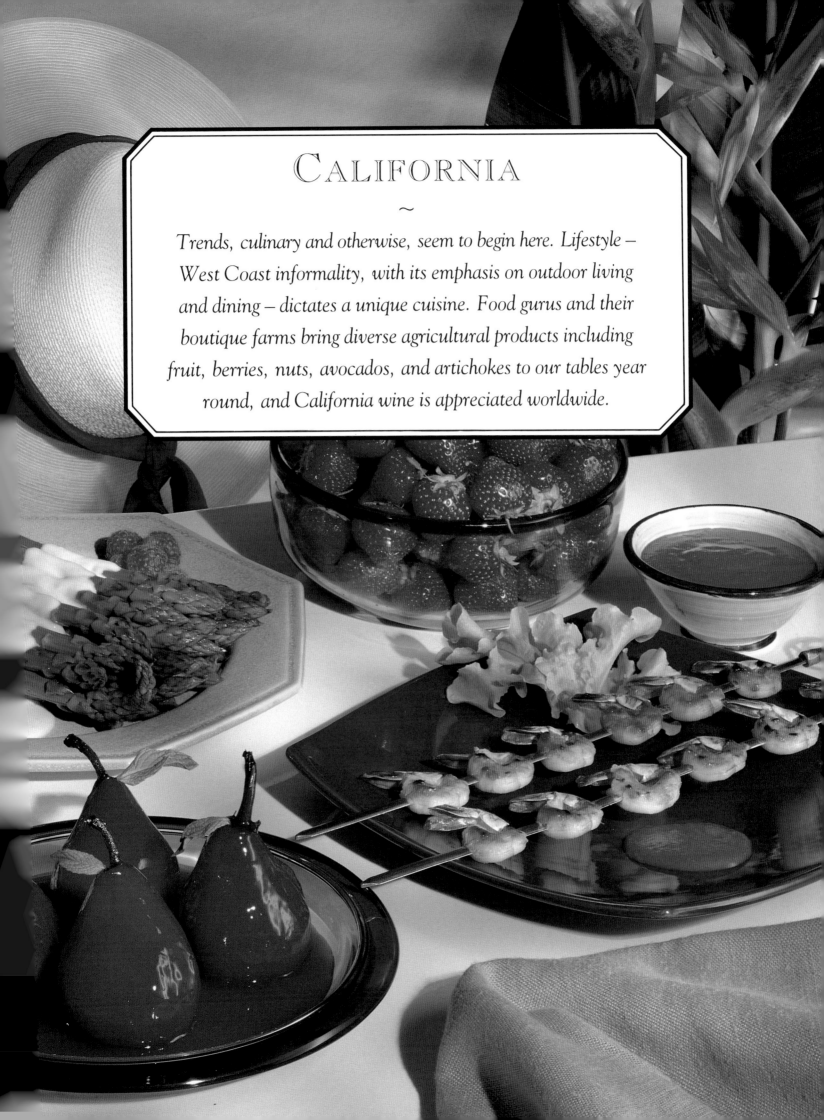

CALIFORNIA

~

Trends, culinary and otherwise, seem to begin here. Lifestyle – West Coast informality, with its emphasis on outdoor living and dining – dictates a unique cuisine. Food gurus and their boutique farms bring diverse agricultural products including fruit, berries, nuts, avocados, and artichokes to our tables year round, and California wine is appreciated worldwide.

Tomato Sandwiches with Olive Mayonnaise

SERVES 6

1 garlic clove, minced

2 tablespoons olive oil

1 teaspoon red wine vinegar

2 beefsteak tomatoes

½ cup fresh basil leaves or parsley, chopped

¼ teaspoon salt

black pepper

7 brine-cured black olives, pitted and minced

6 tablespoons mayonnaise

12 slices of sourdough bread, lightly toasted

6 large lettuce leaves

1 ▼ Combine the garlic, oil, and vinegar in a small bowl and mix together. Or, shake the ingredients in a screwtop jar until blended. Set this dressing aside.

2 ▲ Core the tomatoes. With a sharp knife, cut 6 shallow lengthwise slits in the skin of each to make the tomatoes easier to eat; do not cut too deeply into the flesh. Cut the tomatoes crosswise into thin slices.

3 Place the tomato slices in a shallow dish. Add the oil and vinegar dressing, basil or parsley, salt, and pepper to taste. Let marinate at least 30 minutes.

4 ▲ In another bowl, stir together the olives and mayonnaise.

5 ▲ Spread 6 slices of bread with the olive mayonnaise. Arrange the tomato slices on top and drizzle over any remaining dressing from the bowl. Top each with a lettuce leaf. Cover with the remaining bread and serve.

Gazpacho

SERVES 4

½ hothouse cucumber (about 8 ounces), coarsely chopped

½ green bell pepper, seeded and coarsely chopped

½ red bell pepper, seeded and coarsely chopped

1 large tomato, coarsely chopped

2 scallions, chopped

hot pepper sauce (optional)

3 tablespoons chopped fresh parsley or coriander (cilantro)

croutons, for serving

FOR THE SOUP BASE

1 pound ripe tomatoes, peeled, seeded, and chopped

1 tablespoon ketchup

2 tablespoons tomato paste

¼ teaspoon sugar

¾ teaspoon salt

1 teaspoon pepper

¼ cup sherry vinegar

¾ cup olive oil

1½ cups tomato juice

2 Add the ketchup, tomato paste, sugar, salt, pepper, vinegar, and oil and pulse on and off 3–4 times, just to blend. Transfer to a large bowl. Stir in the tomato juice.

3 ▼ Place the cucumber and bell peppers in the food processor or blender and pulse on and off until finely chopped; do not overmix.

4 ▲ Reserve about 2 tablespoons of the chopped vegetables for garnishing; stir the remainder into the soup base. Taste for seasoning. Mix in the chopped tomato, scallions, and a dash of hot pepper sauce if desired. Chill well.

5 To serve, ladle into bowls and sprinkle with the reserved chopped vegetables, chopped fresh parsley or coriander, and croutons.

1 ▲ For the soup base, put the tomatoes in a food processor or blender and pulse on and off until just smooth, scraping the sides of the container occasionally.

Individual Goat Cheese Tarts

SERVES 6

6–8 sheets phyllo pastry (about 4 ounces)

4 tablespoons butter, melted

12 ounces firm log-shaped goat cheese, rind removed

9 cherry tomatoes, quartered

½ cup milk

2 eggs

2 tablespoons whipping cream

⅛ teaspoon ground white pepper

~ COOK'S TIP ~

Keep the phyllo pastry under a damp cloth while working to prevent the sheets from drying out.

1 Preheat the oven to 375°F. Grease 6 4-inch tartlet pans.

2 ▲ For one pan, cut out 4 circles of phyllo pastry, each about 4½ inches in diameter. Place one circle in the pan and brush with butter. Top with another phyllo circle and brush with butter. Continue until there are 4 layers of phyllo; do not butter the last layer. Repeat the procedure for the remaining pans.

3 ▲ Place the pastry-lined pans on a baking sheet. Cut the goat cheese log into 6 slices. Place a slice in each of the pastry shells.

4 ▲ Arrange the tomato quarters around the cheese slices.

5 ▲ Combine the milk, eggs, cream, and pepper in a measure or bowl and whisk to mix. Pour into the pastry shells, filling them almost to the top.

6 Bake until puffed and golden, 30–40 minutes. Serve hot or warm, with a mixed green salad if desired.

Turkey and Avocado Pita Pizzas

SERVES 4

| 8 plum tomatoes, quartered |
| 3–4 tablespoons olive oil |
| salt and pepper |
| 1 large ripe avocado |
| 8 pita bread rounds |
| 6–7 slices of cooked turkey, chopped |
| 1 onion, thinly sliced |
| 2½ cups shredded Monterey Jack cheese |
| 2 tablespoons chopped fresh coriander (cilantro) |

1 Preheat the oven to 450°F.

2 ▲ Place the tomatoes in a baking dish. Drizzle over 1 tablespoon of the oil and season with salt and pepper. Bake 30 minutes; do not stir.

3 Remove the baking dish from the oven and mash the tomatoes with a fork, removing the skins as you mash. Set aside.

4 ▲ Peel and pit the avocado. Cut into 16 thin slices.

5 Brush the edges of the pita breads with oil. Arrange the breads on 2 baking sheets.

6 ▼ Spread each pita with mashed tomato, almost to the edges.

7 ▲ Top each with 2 avocado slices. Sprinkle with the turkey, then add a few onion slices. Season with salt and pepper. Sprinkle on the cheese.

8 Place one sheet in the middle of the oven and bake until the cheese begins to melt, 15–20 minutes. Sprinkle with half the coriander and serve. Meanwhile, bake the second batch of pizzas to serve them hot.

Crab Louis

SERVES 4

4 cups Boston or Bibb lettuce leaves

2 cups fresh lump crab meat

4 hard-cooked eggs, sliced

4 tomatoes, quartered

½ green bell pepper, seeded and thinly
    sliced

½ cup pitted black olives, sliced

FOR THE DRESSING

1 cup mayonnaise

2 teaspoons fresh lemon juice

¼ cup chili sauce

½ green bell pepper, seeded and minced

1 teaspoon prepared horseradish

1 teaspoon Worcestershire sauce

1 ▲ For the dressing, combine all
the ingredients in a bowl and mix
well. Set aside.

2 Line 4 salad plates with the lettuce
leaves. Mound the crab meat in the
center. Arrange hard-cooked eggs and
tomatoes around the outside.

3 ▼ Spoon some of the dressing over
the crab. Arrange the green pepper
slices on top and sprinkle with the
olives. Serve immediately, with the
remaining dressing.

Poolside Tuna Salad

SERVES 4–6

6 ounces radishes

1 hothouse cucumber

3 celery stalks

1 yellow bell pepper

6 ounces cherry tomatoes, halved

4 scallions, thinly sliced

½ teaspoon salt, or to taste

¼ cup fresh lemon juice

¼ cup olive oil

black pepper

2 7-ounce cans tuna, drained

2 tablespoons chopped fresh parsley

lettuce leaves, for serving

twisted lemon peel, for garnishing

1 Cut the radishes, cucumber, celery,
and bell pepper into pea-sized dice.
Place in a large, shallow dish. Add the
tomatoes and scallions.

2 ▼ In a small bowl, stir together the
salt and lemon juice with a fork until
dissolved. Pour this over the vegetable
mixture. Add the oil and pepper to
taste. Stir to blend. Cover and let
stand 1 hour.

3 Add the tuna and parsley and toss
gently until combined.

4 ▲ Arrange lettuce leaves on a
platter and mound the salad in the
center. Garnish with the lemon peel.

> ### ~ VARIATION ~
>
> Prepare the vegetables as above
> and add the parsley. Arrange
> lettuce leaves on individual plates
> and divide the vegetable mixture
> among them. Place a mound of
> tuna on top of each and finish
> with a dollop of mayonnaise.

Crab Louis (top), Poolside Tuna Salad

Goat Cheese Salad

SERVES 4

2 tablespoons olive oil

4 slices of French bread, ½ inch thick

8 cups mixed salad greens, such as curly endive, radicchio, and red oak leaf, torn in small pieces

4 firm goat cheese rounds, about 2 ounces each, rind removed

1 yellow or red bell pepper, seeded and finely diced

1 small red onion, thinly sliced

3 tablespoons chopped fresh parsley

2 tablespoons chopped fresh chives

FOR THE DRESSING

2 tablespoons wine vinegar

¼ teaspoon salt

1 teaspoon whole-grain mustard

5 tablespoons olive oil

black pepper

1 For the dressing, mix the vinegar and salt with a fork until dissolved. Stir in the mustard. Gradually stir in the oil until blended. Season with pepper and set aside.

2 Preheat the broiler.

3 ▲ Heat the oil in a skillet. When hot, add the bread slices and cook until golden, about 1 minute. Turn and cook the other side, about 30 seconds more. Drain on paper towels and set aside.

4 ▲ Place the salad greens in a bowl. Add 3 tablespoons of the dressing and toss to coat. Divide the dressed leaves among 4 salad plates.

5 ▲ Put the goat cheeses, cut side up, on a baking sheet and broil until bubbling and golden, 1–2 minutes.

6 Set 1 goat cheese on each slice of bread and place in the center of each plate. Scatter the diced bell pepper, red onion, parsley, and chives over the salad. Drizzle with the remaining dressing and serve.

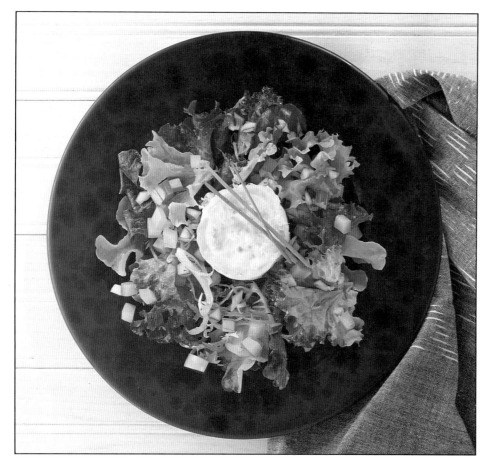

~ **VARIATION** ~

For a more substantial main course salad, increase the amount of greens and make double the quantity of dressing. Add 2 cups sliced cooked green beans and 2 cups slivered or diced ham to the greens, and toss with half of the dressing. Top with broiled goat cheeses and remaining dressing.

Three-Bean and Lentil Salad

SERVES 6

1 cup dried garbanzo beans (chick peas), soaked overnight and drained

1 cup dried red kidney beans, soaked overnight and drained

3 bay leaves

2 tablespoons coarse salt

½ cup lentils

8 ounces fresh green beans, cut in 1-inch slices and cooked

1 small red onion, minced

3 scallions, chopped

1 tablespoon chopped fresh parsley

FOR THE DRESSING

5–6 tablespoons red wine vinegar

1 teaspoon salt

2 teaspoons Dijon-style mustard

6 tablespoons olive oil

1 garlic clove, minced

black pepper

3 Halfway through the beans' cooking time, put the lentils in a large pot and add cold water to cover and the remaining bay leaf. Bring to a boil, then cover and simmer until just tender, 30–40 minutes.

4 ▼ As the lentils and the beans finish cooking, drain thoroughly in a colander and place them in a large bowl. Discard the bay leaves.

5 ▲ Add the green beans, red onion, scallions, and parsley to the bowl. Add the dressing and toss well.

6 Taste the salad and adjust the seasoning, adding more vinegar, salt, and pepper if desired. Serve at room temperature.

1 ▲ For the dressing, in a bowl mix 4 tablespoons of the vinegar and the salt with a fork until dissolved. Stir in the mustard. Gradually stir in the oil until blended. Add the garlic and pepper to taste. Set aside.

2 Put the garbanzo beans and kidney beans in separate large pots. To each, add fresh cold water to cover and 1 bay leaf. Bring to a boil, then cover and simmer 30 minutes. Add 1 tablespoon coarse salt to each pot and continue simmering until tender, 30 minutes–1½ hours more.

Artichoke Pasta Salad

SERVES 4

7 tablespoons olive oil

1 red bell pepper, quartered, seeded, and thinly sliced

1 onion, halved and thinly sliced

1 teaspoon dried thyme

salt and pepper

3 tablespoons sherry vinegar

1 pound pasta shapes, such as penne or fusilli

2 6-ounce jars marinated artichoke hearts, drained and thinly sliced

5 ounces cooked broccoli, chopped

20–25 salt-cured black olives, pitted and chopped

2 tablespoons chopped fresh parsley

1 ▼ Heat 2 tablespoons of the oil in a nonstick skillet. Add the red bell pepper and onion and cook over low heat until just soft, 8–10 minutes, stirring occasionally.

2 ▲ Stir in the thyme, ¼ teaspoon salt, and the vinegar. Cook, stirring, 30 seconds more, then set aside.

3 ▲ Bring a large pot of salted water to a boil. Add the pasta and cook until just tender (check package directions for timing). Drain, rinse with hot water, then drain again well. Transfer to a large bowl. Add 2 tablespoons of the oil and toss well to coat.

4 ▲ Add the artichokes, broccoli, olives, parsley, onion mixture, and remaining oil to the pasta. Season with salt and pepper. Stir to blend. Let stand at least 1 hour before serving, or refrigerate overnight. Serve at room temperature.

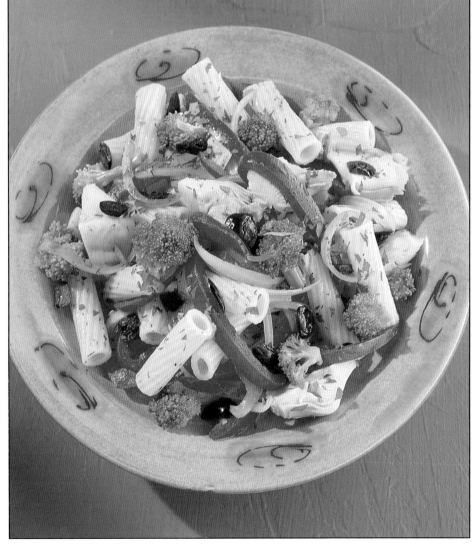

Asparagus with Creamy Raspberry Vinaigrette

SERVES 4

1½ pounds thin asparagus spears

2 tablespoons raspberry vinegar

½ teaspoon salt

1 teaspoon Dijon-style mustard

5 tablespoons sunflower oil

2 tablespoons sour cream or plain yogurt

white pepper

1 cup fresh raspberries

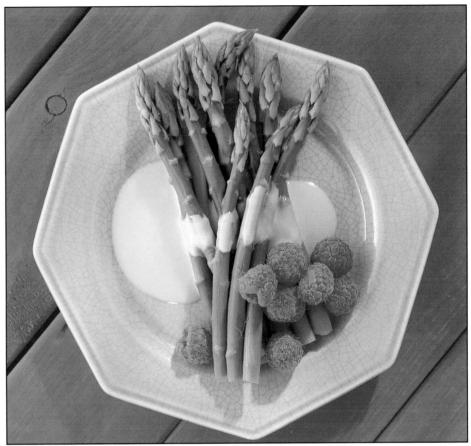

1 Fill a large wide pot, frying pan, or wok with water about 4 inches deep and bring to a boil.

2 ▲ Trim the tough ends of the asparagus spears. If desired, remove the "scales" using a vegetable peeler.

3 ▲ Tie the asparagus spears into 2 bundles. Lower the bundles into the boiling water and cook until just tender, about 2 minutes.

4 ▼ With a slotted spatula, carefully remove the asparagus bundles from the boiling water and immerse in cold water to stop the cooking. Drain and untie the bundles. Pat dry with paper towels. Refrigerate the asparagus at least 1 hour.

5 ▲ Combine the vinegar and salt in a bowl and stir with a fork until dissolved. Stir in the mustard. Gradually stir in the oil until blended. Add the sour cream or yogurt and pepper to taste.

6 To serve, place the asparagus on individual plates and drizzle the dressing across the middle of the spears. Garnish with the fresh raspberries and serve.

California Taco Salad with Beef

SERVES 4

2 teaspoons vegetable oil

1 pound lean ground beef

1 small onion, chopped

½ teaspoon salt

¼ teaspoon cayenne, or to taste

1 cup corn kernels (fresh, frozen, or canned)

1 cup cooked or canned kidney beans

1 tablespoon chopped fresh coriander (cilantro), plus more coriander leaves for garnishing

1 small head of romaine lettuce

3 tomatoes, quartered

2 cups shredded Monterey Jack or cheddar cheese

1 avocado

⅓ cup pitted black olives, sliced

4 scallions, chopped

tortilla chips, for serving

FOR THE DRESSING

3 tablespoons white wine vinegar

½ teaspoon salt

1 teaspoon Dijon-style mustard

2 tablespoons buttermilk

⅔ cup vegetable oil

1 small garlic clove, minced

1 teaspoon ground cumin

1 teaspoon dried oregano

¼ teaspoon pepper

~ VARIATIONS ~

For California Taco Salad with Chicken, substitute 1 pound boneless, skinless chicken breast, finely diced, for the ground beef. Garbanzo beans (chick peas) may be used in place of kidney beans. Although frozen or canned corn is convenient, freshly cooked corn kernels scraped from the cob give added moisture and extra flavor.

1 ▲ For the dressing, mix the vinegar and salt with a fork until dissolved. Stir in the mustard and buttermilk. Gradually stir in the oil until blended. Add the garlic, cumin, oregano, and pepper and set aside.

2 ▲ Heat the oil in a nonstick skillet. Add the beef, onion, salt, and cayenne and cook until just browned, 5–7 minutes. Stir frequently to break up lumps. Drain and let cool.

3 ▲ In a large bowl, combine the beef, corn, kidney beans, and chopped coriander and toss to blend.

4 ▲ Stack the lettuce leaves on top of one another and slice thinly, crosswise, into shreds. Place in another bowl and toss with ¼ cup of the dressing. Divide the lettuce among 4 dinner plates.

5 ▲ Mound the meat mixture in the center of each plate. Arrange the tomatoes at the edge. Sprinkle with the shredded cheese.

6 ▲ Peel, pit, and dice the avocado. Scatter on top of the salad together with the olives and scallions.

7 Pour the remaining dressing over the salads. Garnish with coriander. Serve with tortilla chips.

Zucchini-Cheese Casserole

1 garlic clove, crushed with a knife

2 tablespoons olive oil or melted butter

2 pounds zucchini

salt and pepper

2 cups shredded Monterey Jack cheese

2 eggs

1½ cups milk

~ VARIATION ~

For a spicier version, replace the cheese with Jalapeño Jack cheese, and toss the zucchini with 2 teaspoons chili powder.

1 Preheat the oven to 375°F.

2 ▼ Rub the garlic clove around the inside of a baking dish, pressing hard to extract the juice; discard the garlic. Grease the dish with half the oil or melted butter.

3 ▲ Cut the zucchini across into ¼-inch slices. Place them in a bowl and toss with the remaining oil or melted butter and salt to taste.

4 ▲ Arrange half the zucchini slices in an even layer in the baking dish. Sprinkle with half the cheese. Add the remaining zucchini, spreading it evenly on the top.

5 ▲ Combine the eggs, milk, ½ teaspoon salt, and pepper to taste in a bowl and whisk together. Pour over the zucchini. Sprinkle with the remaining cheese.

6 Cover with foil and bake about 30 minutes. Remove the foil and continue baking until the top is browned, 30–40 minutes more. Serve hot, warm, or cold.

San Francisco Chicken Wings

SERVES 4

⅓ cup soy sauce
1 tablespoon light brown sugar
1 tablespoon rice vinegar
2 tablespoons dry sherry wine
juice of 1 orange
2-inch strip of orange peel
1 star anise
1 teaspoon cornstarch
¼ cup water
1 tablespoon minced fresh gingerroot
¼–1 teaspoon Oriental chili-garlic sauce, to taste
3½ pounds chicken wings (22–24), tips removed

1 Preheat the oven to 400°F.

2 ▲ Combine the soy sauce, brown sugar, vinegar, sherry, orange juice and peel, and star anise in a saucepan. Bring to a boil over medium heat.

3 ▲ Combine the cornstarch and water in a small bowl and stir until blended. Add to the boiling soy sauce mixture, stirring well. Boil 1 minute more, stirring constantly.

4 ▼ Remove the soy sauce mixture from the heat and stir in the minced ginger and chili-garlic sauce.

5 ▲ Arrange the chicken wings, in one layer, in a large baking dish. Pour over the soy sauce mixture and stir to coat the wings evenly.

6 Bake until tender and browned, 30–40 minutes, basting occasionally. Serve the wings hot or warm.

Swordfish with Bell Pepper-Orange Relish

SERVES 4

5 tablespoons olive oil

1 large fennel bulb, cut in ¼-inch dice

1 red bell pepper, seeded and cut in ¼-inch dice

1 yellow bell pepper, seeded and cut in ¼-inch dice

1 orange or green bell pepper, seeded and cut in ¼-inch dice

1 small onion, cut in ¼-inch dice

1 teaspoon grated orange rind

¼ cup fresh orange juice

salt

4 pieces of swordfish steak, about 5 ounces each

1 ▼ Heat 3 tablespoons of the oil in a large nonstick skillet. Add the fennel, bell peppers, and onion and cook over medium heat until just tender, about 5 minutes (they should retain some crunch).

2 ▲ Stir in the orange rind and juice and cook 1 minute more. Stir in ½ teaspoon salt. Cover and set aside.

3 Bring some water to a boil in the bottom of a steamer.

4 ▲ Meanwhile, brush the fish steaks on both sides with the remaining oil and season with salt.

5 ▲ Place the fish steaks in the top part of the steamer. Cover the pan and steam until the steaks are opaque throughout, about 5 minutes.

6 Transfer the fish to dinner plates. Serve immediately, accompanied by the bell pepper relish.

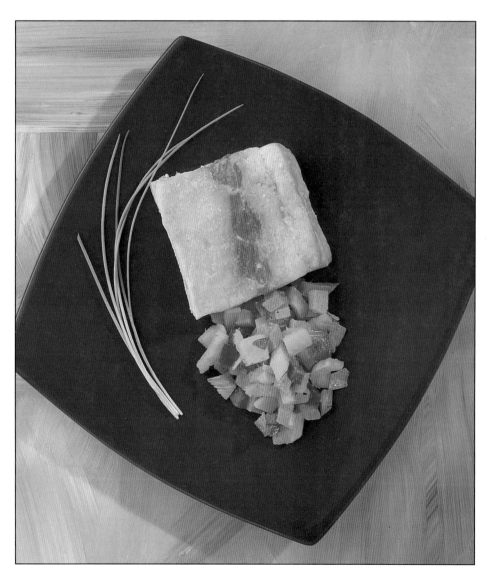

Tangerine-Soy Marinated Salmon

SERVES 4

1 cup soy sauce

1½ teaspoons firmly packed brown sugar

¼ cup rice vinegar

1 tablespoon minced fresh gingerroot

2 garlic cloves, minced

grated rind and juice of 1 tangerine

½ cup water

4 pieces of salmon fillet, about 6 ounces each

1 ▲ Combine the soy sauce, sugar, vinegar, ginger, garlic, orange rind and juice, and water in a bowl. Stir until well blended.

2 ▲ Arrange the fish, in one layer, in a large shallow dish. Pour over the soy sauce mixture and turn the fish so that both sides are coated. Cover and let marinate at room temperature 1 hour, or refrigerate overnight.

3 Preheat the oven to 350°F.

4 ▼ Remove the fish from the marinade, leaving on any pieces of ginger that cling to the fish. Place in a baking dish, in one layer.

5 ▲ Cover the dish with foil. Bake until the fish is opaque throughout, 20–30 minutes. Transfer to dinner plates and serve immediately. Good served with steamed broccoli.

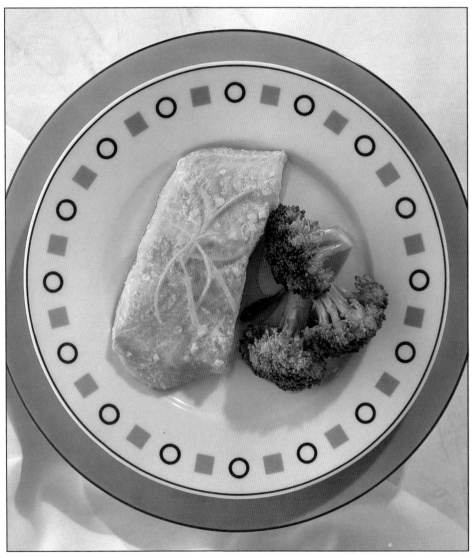

Cioppino

SERVES 4

1½ tablespoons olive oil

1 onion, halved and thinly sliced

several saffron threads, crushed

1 teaspoon dried thyme

⅛ teaspoon cayenne

salt and pepper

2 garlic cloves, minced

1 28-ounce can peeled tomatoes, drained and chopped

¾ cup dry white wine

2 quarts fish stock

12 ounces skinless fish fillets, cut into pieces

1 pound monkfish, membrane removed, cut into pieces

1 pound mussels in shell, thoroughly scrubbed

½ pound small squid bodies, cleaned and cut in rings

2 tablespoons chopped fresh parsley

thickly sliced sourdough bread, for serving

1 ▼ Heat the oil in a large, heavy pot. Add the onion, saffron, thyme, cayenne, and ½ teaspoon salt. Stir well and cook over low heat until soft, 8–10 minutes. Add the garlic and cook 1 minute more.

~ COOK'S TIP ~

Do not prepare mussels more than a few hours in advance of cooking or they will spoil and die.

2 ▲ Stir in the tomatoes, wine, and fish stock. Bring to a boil and boil 1 minute, then reduce the heat to medium-low and simmer 15 minutes.

3 ▲ Add the fish fillet and monkfish pieces to the pot and simmer gently 3 minutes.

4 ▲ Add the mussels and squid and simmer until the mussel shells open, about 2 minutes more. Stir in the parsley. Season with salt and pepper.

5 Ladle into warmed soup bowls and serve immediately, with bread.

Shrimp Kabobs with Plum Sauce

SERVES 6

1 tablespoon vegetable oil

1 onion, minced

1 garlic clove, minced

1 pound purple plums, pitted and chopped

1 tablespoon rice vinegar

2 tablespoons fresh orange juice

1 teaspoon Dijon-style mustard

2 tablespoons soy sauce

1 tablespoon firmly packed light brown sugar

1 point of a star anise

½ cup water

1½ pounds medium-size raw shrimp, peeled (tails left on if desired) and deveined

boiled rice, for serving

1 ▲ Heat the oil in a saucepan. Add the onion, garlic, and plums and cook over low heat, stirring occasionally, until softened, about 10 minutes.

2 Stir in the vinegar, orange juice, mustard, soy sauce, sugar, star anise, and water. Bring to a boil. Lower the heat, cover, and simmer, stirring occasionally, 20 minutes.

3 Uncover the pan and simmer the sauce 10 minutes more to thicken, stirring frequently.

4 ▼ Remove the star anise. Transfer to a food processor or blender and purée until smooth.

5 Press the sauce through a fine strainer to remove all the fibers and plum skins.

6 Preheat the broiler.

7 ▲ Thread the shrimp, flat, onto 6 skewers. Brush them all over with three-quarters of the plum sauce.

8 Place the shrimp kabobs on the foil-lined broiler pan. Broil until opaque throughout, 5–6 minutes. Turn the kabobs once.

9 Meanwhile, reheat the remaining plum sauce. Serve the kabobs with rice and the sauce.

Lemon Chicken with Guacamole Sauce

SERVES 4

juice of 2 lemons

3 tablespoons olive oil

2 garlic cloves, minced

salt and pepper

4 chicken breast halves, about 7 ounces each

2 beefsteak tomatoes, cored and cut in half

chopped fresh coriander (cilantro), for garnishing

FOR THE SAUCE

1 ripe avocado

¼ cup sour cream

3 tablespoons fresh lemon juice

½ teaspoon salt

¼ cup water

1 ▲ Combine the lemon juice, oil, garlic, ½ teaspoon salt, and a little pepper in a bowl. Stir to mix.

> ### ~ VARIATION ~
>
> To grill the chicken, prepare the fire, and when the coals are glowing red and covered with grey ash, spread them in a single layer. Set an oiled grill rack about 5 inches above the coals and cook the chicken breasts until lightly charred and cooked through, about 15–20 minutes. Allow extra olive oil for basting.

2 ▲ Arrange the chicken breasts, in one layer, in a shallow glass or ceramic dish. Pour over the lemon mixture and turn to coat evenly. Cover and let stand at least 1 hour at room temperature, or refrigerate overnight.

3 ▲ For the sauce, cut the avocado in half, remove the pit, and scrape the flesh into a food processor or blender.

4 ▲ Add the sour cream, lemon juice, and salt and process until smooth. Add the water and process just to blend. If necessary, add more water to thin the sauce. Transfer to a bowl, taste and adjust the seasoning, if necessary. Set aside.

5 ▲ Preheat the broiler. Heat a ridged grill pan. Remove the chicken from the marinade and pat dry.

6 ▲ When the grill pan is hot, add the chicken breasts and cook, turning often, until they are cooked through, about 10 minutes.

7 ▲ Meanwhile, arrange the tomato halves, cut-sides up, on a baking sheet and season lightly with salt and pepper. Broil until hot and bubbling, about 5 minutes.

8 To serve, place a chicken breast, tomato half, and a dollop of avocado sauce on each plate. Sprinkle with coriander and serve.

Cornish Hens with Raisin-Walnut Stuffing

SERVES 4

1 cup Port wine
⅔ cup raisins
1 tablespoon walnut oil
3 ounces mushrooms, minced
1 large celery stalk, minced
1 small onion, chopped
salt and pepper
1 cup fresh bread crumbs
½ cup chopped walnuts
1 tablespoon each chopped fresh basil and parsley, or 2 tablespoons chopped parsley
½ teaspoon dried thyme
6 tablespoons butter, melted
4 Cornish hens

1 Preheat the oven to 350°F.

2 In a small bowl, combine the Port wine and raisins and let soak about 20 minutes.

3 ▲ Meanwhile, heat the oil in a nonstick skillet. Add the mushrooms, celery, onion, and ¼ teaspoon salt and cook over low heat until softened, 8–10 minutes. Let cool slightly.

4 ▲ Drain the raisins, reserving the Port. Combine the raisins, bread crumbs, walnuts, basil, parsley, and thyme in a bowl. Stir in the onion mixture and 4 tablespoons of the butter. Add ½ teaspoon salt and pepper to taste.

5 ▲ Fill the cavity of each hen with the stuffing mixture. Do not pack down. Tie the legs together, looping the tail with the string to enclose the stuffing securely.

6 Brush the hens with the remaining butter and place in a baking dish just large enough to hold the birds comfortably. Pour over the reserved Port wine.

7 Roast, basting occasionally, about 1 hour. To test for doneness, pierce the thigh with a skewer; the juices should run clear. Serve immediately, pouring some of the pan juices over each bird.

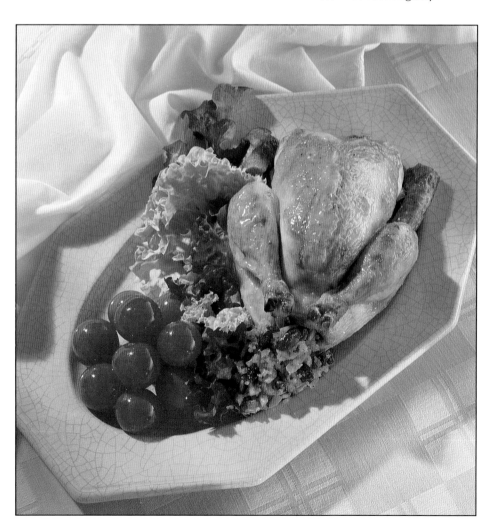

Fusilli with Turkey, Tomatoes, and Broccoli

SERVES 4

1½ pounds ripe but firm plum tomatoes, quartered

6 tablespoons olive oil

1 teaspoon dried oregano

salt and pepper

12 ounces broccoli florets

1 small onion, sliced

1 teaspoon dried thyme

1 pound skinless boneless turkey breast, cubed

3 garlic cloves, minced

1 tablespoon fresh lemon juice

1 pound fusilli

1 Preheat the oven to 400°F.

2 ▲ Place the tomatoes in a baking dish. Add 1 tablespoon oil, the oregano, and ½ teaspoon salt and stir to blend.

3 Bake until the tomatoes are just browned, 30–40 minutes; do not stir.

4 Meanwhile, bring a large pot of salted water to a boil. Add the broccoli and cook until just tender, about 5 minutes. Drain and set aside. (Alternatively, steam the broccoli until tender.)

5 ▲ Heat 2 tablespoons of the oil in a large nonstick skillet. Add the onion, thyme, cubes of turkey, and ½ teaspoon salt. Cook over high heat, stirring often, until the meat is cooked and beginning to brown, 5–7 minutes. Add the garlic and cook 1 minute more, stirring frequently.

6 Remove from the heat. Stir in the lemon juice and season with pepper. Set aside and keep warm.

7 Bring another large pot of salted water to a boil. Add the fusilli and cook until just tender (check package directions for timing). Drain and place in a large bowl. Toss with the remaining oil.

8 ▼ Add the broccoli to the turkey mixture. Add to the fusilli. Add the tomatoes and stir gently to blend. Serve immediately.

Chicken with White Wine, Olives, and Garlic

SERVES 4

3½-pound chicken, cut in serving
   pieces

1 onion, sliced

salt and pepper

3–6 garlic cloves, to taste, minced

1 teaspoon dried thyme

2 cups dry white California wine

1 cup green olives (16–18), pitted

1 bay leaf

1 tablespoon lemon juice

1–2 tablespoons butter

1 Heat a deep, heavy castiron skillet. When hot, add the chicken pieces, skin side down, and cook over medium heat until browned, about 10 minutes. Turn and brown the other side, 5–8 minutes more. (Work in batches if necessary.)

2 Transfer the chicken pieces to a platter and set aside.

3 Drain the excess fat from the skillet, leaving about 1 tablespoon. Add the onion and ½ teaspoon salt and cook until just soft, about 5 minutes. Add the garlic and thyme and cook 1 minute more.

4 ▼ Add the wine and stir, scraping up any bits that cling to the pan. Bring to a boil and boil 1 minute. Stir in the green olives.

5 ▲ Return the chicken pieces to the pan. Add the bay leaf and season lightly with pepper. Lower the heat, cover, and simmer until the chicken is cooked through, 20–30 minutes.

6 Transfer the chicken pieces to a warmed platter. Stir the lemon juice into the sauce. Whisk in the butter to thicken the sauce slightly. Spoon over the chicken and serve immediately.

Turkey Meat Loaf

SERVES 4

1 tablespoon olive oil

1 onion, chopped

1 green bell pepper, seeded and minced

1 garlic clove, minced

1 pound ground turkey

1 cup fresh bread crumbs

1 egg, beaten

½ cup pine nuts

12 sun-dried tomatoes in oil, drained
   and chopped

⅓ cup milk

2 teaspoons chopped fresh rosemary, or
   ½ teaspoon dried rosemary

1 teaspoon ground fennel

½ teaspoon dried oregano

½ teaspoon salt

1 Preheat the oven to 375°F.

2 ▼ Heat the oil in a skillet. Add the onion, bell pepper, and garlic and cook over low heat, stirring often, until just softened, 8–10 minutes. Remove from the heat and let cool.

3 Place the turkey in a large bowl. Add the onion mixture and the remaining ingredients and mix thoroughly together.

4 ▲ Transfer to an 8½- × 4½-inch loaf pan, packing the mixture down firmly. Bake until golden brown, about 1 hour. Serve hot or cold.

Chicken with White Wine, Olives, and Garlic (top), Turkey Meat Loaf

Pork Chops with Chili-Nectarine Relish

1 cup fresh orange juice

3 tablespoons olive oil

2 garlic cloves, minced

1 teaspoon ground cumin

1 tablespoon coarsely ground black pepper

8 pork loin chops, about ¾ inch thick, well trimmed

salt

FOR THE RELISH

1 small fresh green chili pepper

2 tablespoons honey

juice of ½ lemon

1 cup chicken stock

2 nectarines, pitted and chopped

1 garlic clove, minced

½ onion, minced

1 teaspoon minced fresh gingerroot

¼ teaspoon salt

1 tablespoon chopped fresh coriander (cilantro)

1 For the relish, roast the chili over a gas flame, holding it with tongs, until charred on all sides. (Alternatively, char the skin under the broiler.) Let cool 5 minutes.

2 ▼ Wearing rubber gloves, carefully remove the charred skin of the chili. Discard seeds if a less hot flavor is desired. Mince the chili and place in a heavy saucepan.

3 ▲ Add the honey, lemon juice, chicken stock, nectarines, garlic, onion, ginger, and salt. Bring to a boil, then simmer, stirring occasionally, about 30 minutes. Stir in the coriander and set aside.

4 In a small bowl, combine the orange juice, oil, garlic, cumin, and pepper. Stir to mix.

5 ▲ Arrange the pork chops, in one layer, in a shallow dish. Pour over the orange juice mixture and turn to coat. Cover and let stand at least 1 hour, or refrigerate overnight.

6 Remove the pork from the marinade and pat dry with paper towels. Season lightly with salt.

7 Heat a ridged grill pan. When hot, add the pork chops and cook until browned, about 5 minutes. Turn and cook on the other side until done, about 10 minutes more. (Work in batches if necessary.) Serve immediately, with the relish.

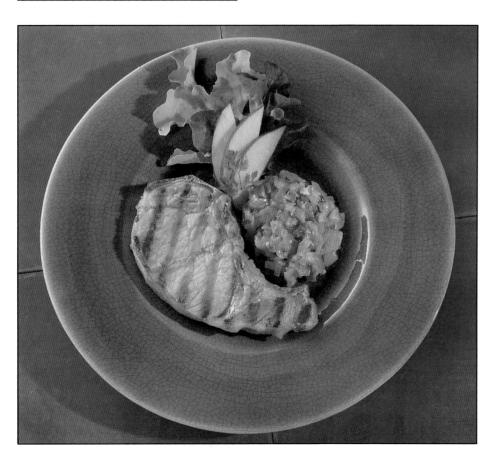

Roast Leg of Lamb with Pesto

SERVES 6

2 cups fresh basil leaves
4 garlic cloves, coarsely chopped
3 tablespoons pine nuts
⅔ cup olive oil
⅔ cup freshly grated Parmesan cheese
1 teaspoon salt, or to taste
5- to 6-pound leg of lamb

1 ▲ To make the pesto, combine the basil, garlic, and pine nuts in a food processor, and process until finely chopped. With the motor running, slowly add the oil in a steady stream.

2 Scrape the mixture into a bowl. Stir in the Parmesan and salt.

3 ▲ Set the lamb in a roasting pan. Make several slits in the meat with a sharp knife and spoon some pesto into each slit.

4 Rub more pesto over the surface of the lamb.

5 ▲ Continue patting on the pesto in a thick, even layer. Cover and let stand 2 hours at room temperature, or refrigerate overnight.

6 Preheat the oven to 350°F.

7 Place the lamb in the oven and roast, allowing about 20 minutes per pound for rare meat, 25 minutes per pound for medium-rare. Turn the lamb occasionally during roasting.

8 Remove the leg of lamb from the oven, cover it loosely with foil, and let rest about 15 minutes before carving and serving.

Beef and Eggplant Stir-Fry with Ginger

SERVES 4–6

1⅓ pounds boneless beef, such as flank
    steak, thinly sliced

2 tablespoons soy sauce, plus extra for
    serving

1 pound eggplant

3 tablespoons water

2 tablespoons rice vinegar

1 tablespoon dry sherry wine

1 teaspoon honey

1 teaspoon red pepper flakes

¼ cup vegetable oil

3 teaspoons sesame oil

1 garlic clove, minced

1 tablespoon minced fresh gingerroot

boiled rice, for serving

1 ▲ Combine the beef and soy sauce
in a shallow dish. Stir to coat evenly.
Cover and let marinate 1 hour, or
refrigerate overnight.

~ VARIATIONS ~

For Turkey and Eggplant Stir-Fry,
substitute thinly sliced turkey
breast for the beef. If time is short,
it is not essential to precook the
eggplant, but microwaving or
steaming the eggplant before stir-
frying helps to eliminate any
bitterness and also prevents the
eggplant from soaking up too
much oil.

---

2 ▲ Cut the eggplant into eighths
lengthwise. Trim away the inner part
with the seeds, leaving a flat edge.
Cut the eggplant slices on the
diagonal into diamond shapes that are
about 1 inch wide.

3 ▲ Place the eggplant in a large
microwaveable dish. Stir in the water.
Cover and microwave on high (650
watt) 3 minutes. Stir gently, then
microwave 3 minutes more. Set aside,
still covered. (Alternatively, steam
the eggplant over boiling water until
tender, if preferred.)

4 ▲ In a small bowl, combine the
vinegar, sherry, honey, and pepper
flakes. Stir to mix. Set aside.

5 ▲ Heat 1 tablespoon vegetable oil
and 1 teaspoon sesame oil in a large
nonstick skillet or wok. Add half of
the beef, garlic, and ginger. Cook
over high heat, stirring frequently,
until the beef is just cooked through,
2–3 minutes. Remove to a bowl. Cook
the remaining beef, garlic, and ginger
in the same way. Add to the bowl and
set aside.

6 ▲ Heat the remaining vegetable
and sesame oils in the skillet or wok.
Add the eggplant and cook over
moderate heat until just browned and
tender, about 5 minutes. (Work in 2
batches if necessary.)

7 Return the beef to the skillet or
wok. Stir in the vinegar mixture and
cook just until the liquid is absorbed,
2–3 minutes more. Taste for
seasoning. Serve immediately, with
rice and extra soy sauce.

Berry Salsa

MAKES 3 CUPS

1 fresh jalapeño pepper

½ red onion, minced

2 scallions, chopped

1 tomato, finely diced

1 small yellow bell pepper, seeded and minced

¼ cup chopped fresh coriander (cilantro)

¼ teaspoon salt

1 tablespoon raspberry vinegar

1 tablespoon fresh orange juice

1 teaspoon honey

1 tablespoon olive oil

½ pint strawberries, hulled

½ pint blueberries or blackberries

½ pint raspberries

1 ▼ Wearing rubber gloves, finely mince the jalapeño pepper (discard the seeds and membrane if a less hot flavor is desired. Place the pepper in a medium-size bowl.

2 ▲ Add the red onion, scallions, tomato, bell pepper, and coriander and stir to blend.

3 ▲ In a small bowl, whisk together the salt, vinegar, orange juice, honey, and oil. Pour over the jalapeño mixture and stir well.

4 ▲ Coarsely chop the strawberries. Add to the jalapeño mixture with the other berries and stir to blend. Let stand at room temperature 3 hours.

5 Serve the salsa at room temperature, with grilled fish or poultry.

Fresh Pineapple-Mint Chutney

MAKES 3 CUPS

1 cup raspberry vinegar

1 cup dry white wine

2 cups chopped fresh pineapple (about 1 small pineapple)

1 cup chopped fresh orange flesh (2 medium-size oranges)

1 cup chopped peeled apple

1 red bell pepper, seeded and diced

1½ onions, minced

¼ cup honey

⅛ teaspoon salt

1 whole clove

4 black peppercorns

2 tablespoons chopped fresh mint

1 ▲ In a saucepan, combine the vinegar and wine and bring to a boil. Boil 3 minutes.

2 ▲ Add the remaining ingredients, except the mint, and stir to blend. Simmer gently about 30 minutes, stirring occasionally.

3 Transfer to a strainer set over a bowl and drain, pressing down to extract the liquid. Remove and discard the clove and peppercorns. Set the fruit mixture aside.

4 ▼ Return the strained juice to the pan and boil until reduced by two-thirds. Pour over the fruit mixture.

5 ▲ Stir in the mint. Let the chutney stand 6–8 hours before serving, with pork or lamb dishes.

~ COOK'S TIP ~

The chutney will keep about 1 week in the refrigerator.

Eggplant Ratatouille

SERVES 6

3½ pounds eggplants (about 4)

3 tablespoons olive oil

1 large onion, sliced

salt and pepper

3 garlic cloves, minced

1 28-ounce can peeled plum tomatoes, drained and chopped

2 tablespoons chopped fresh basil, or 1 teaspoon dried basil

fresh basil leaves, for garnishing

1 Cut the eggplants into large cubes. Bring a large pot of salted water to a boil. Add the eggplant and cook 3–4 minutes. Drain thoroughly.

2 ▼ Heat 2 tablespoons of the oil in a large skillet. Add the onion and ¼ teaspoon salt and cook over low heat until just soft, 8–10 minutes.

3 Add the garlic, eggplant, and remaining oil and stir to mix. Cook gently about 5 minutes.

4 ▲ Stir in the tomatoes and basil. Season with salt and pepper. Cover and cook over low heat until the eggplant is very tender, about 30 minutes, stirring occasionally.

5 Sprinkle the ratatouille with fresh basil leaves and serve.

Garlicky Sautéed Zucchini

SERVES 4

6 medium-size zucchini

2 tablespoons olive oil

½ teaspoon salt

4–6 garlic cloves, minced

1 teaspoon dried thyme

1 tablespoon fresh lemon juice

black pepper

~ VARIATION ~

For Pasta with Zucchini Sauce, add 1 large (28-ounce) can of tomatoes packed in juice, roughly chopped, to the browned zucchini instead of the lemon juice. Simmer until thickened, 5–10 minutes longer. Serve with boiled pasta shapes and sprinkle with grated Parmesan cheese, if desired.

1 ▼ Trim the ends of the zucchini, then halve and quarter them lengthwise. Cut into slices about ¾ inch thick.

2 Heat the oil in a large nonstick skillet. Add the zucchini and toss to coat evenly. Add the salt and stir, then leave to cook until browned on one side, about 5 minutes.

3 ▲ Add the garlic and thyme. Shake the pan and turn the zucchini with the aid of a wooden spatula. Continue cooking until golden brown on both sides and tender, about 5 minutes more. Do not let the garlic burn; if necessary, reduce the heat and increase the cooking time slightly.

4 Stir in the lemon juice, season liberally with black pepper, and serve.

Eggplant Ratatouille (top), Garlicky Sautéed Zucchini

Herbed Goat Cheese Dip

10 ounces soft mild goat cheese

½ cup light cream or half and half

2 teaspoons fresh lemon juice

1 tablespoon chopped fresh chives

1 tablespoon chopped fresh parsley

2 tablespoons chopped fresh basil

black pepper

raw or briefly cooked cold vegetables, potato chips, or crackers, for serving

1 ▼ In a food processor or blender, combine the goat cheese and cream and process to blend. Add the lemon juice and process until smooth.

2 ▲ Scrape into a bowl. Stir in the chives, parsley, basil, and pepper to taste. Serve cold, as a dip for vegetables, potato chips, or crackers.

Avocado Dressing

2 tablespoons wine vinegar

½ teaspoon salt, or to taste

¾ teaspoon white pepper

½ red onion, coarsely chopped

3 tablespoons olive oil

1 large ripe avocado, halved and pit removed

1 tablespoon fresh lemon juice

3 tablespoons plain yogurt

3 tablespoons water, or as needed

2 tablespoons chopped fresh coriander (cilantro)

raw or briefly cooked cold vegetables, for serving

~ COOK'S TIP ~

This versatile dressing need not be limited to serving with salads and crudités. Serve it as a sauce with grilled chicken or fish, or use it on sandwiches in place of mayonnaise or mustard, or to provide a cool contrast to any sort of spicy food.

1 ▲ In a bowl, combine the vinegar and salt and stir with a fork to dissolve. Stir in the pepper, chopped red onion, and olive oil.

2 ▲ Scoop the avocado flesh into a food processor or blender. Add the lemon juice and onion dressing and process just to blend.

3 ▲ Add the yogurt and water and process until smooth. If desired, add more water to thin. Taste and adjust the seasoning if necessary.

4 ▲ Scrape into a bowl. Stir in the coriander. Serve immediately, as a dressing for salads, or use as a dip for raw or briefly cooked cold vegetables.

Herbed Goat Cheese Dip (top), Avocado Dressing

Zinfandel Poached Pears

SERVES 4

1 bottle of red Zinfandel wine

¾ cup sugar

3 tablespoons honey

juice of ½ lemon

1 cinnamon stick

1 vanilla bean, split open lengthwise

2-inch piece of orange peel

1 whole clove

1 black peppercorn

4 firm, ripe pears

whipped cream or sour cream, for
serving

1 ▼ In a saucepan just large enough
to hold the pears standing upright,
combine the wine, sugar, honey,
lemon juice, cinnamon, vanilla bean,
orange peel, clove, and peppercorn.
Heat gently, stirring occasionally until
the sugar has dissolved.

2 ▲ Meanwhile, peel the pears,
leaving the core and stem intact. Slice
a small piece off the base of each pear
so it will stand upright.

3 ▲ Gently place the pears in the
wine mixture. Simmer, uncovered,
until the pears are just tender, 20–35
minutes depending on size and
ripeness; do not overcook.

4 ▲ With a slotted spoon, gently
transfer the pears to a bowl. Continue
to boil the poaching liquid until
reduced by about half. Let cool.

5 Strain the cooled liquid over the
pears and refrigerate at least 3 hours.

6 Place the pears in serving dishes
and spoon over the liquid. Serve with
whipped cream or sour cream.

Baked Peaches with Raspberry Sauce

SERVES 6

3 tablespoons unsalted butter, at room temperature

¼ cup sugar

1 egg, beaten

½ cup ground almonds

6 ripe peaches

FOR THE SAUCE

1 cup raspberries

1 tablespoon confectioners' sugar

1 tablespoon fruit-flavored brandy (optional)

1 Preheat the oven to 350°F.

2 ▲ Beat the butter with the sugar until soft and fluffy. Beat in the egg. Add the ground almonds and beat just to blend well together.

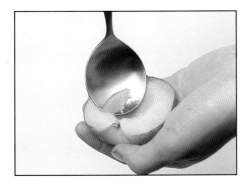

3 ▲ Halve the peaches and remove the pits. With a spoon, scrape out some of the flesh from each peach half, slightly enlarging the hollow left by the pit. Reserve the excess peach flesh to use in the sauce.

4 ▼ Place the peach halves on a baking sheet (if necessary, secure with crumpled foil to keep them steady). Fill the hollow in each peach half with the almond mixture.

5 Bake until the almond filling is puffed and golden and the peaches are very tender, about 30 minutes.

6 ▲ Meanwhile, for the sauce, combine all the ingredients in a food processor or blender. Add the reserved peach flesh. Process until smooth. Press through a strainer set over a bowl to remove fibers and seeds.

7 Let the peaches cool slightly. Place 2 peach halves on each plate and spoon over some of the sauce. Serve immediately.

Chocolate, Coconut, and Macadamia Parfait

SERVES 10

8 ounces white chocolate, chopped

2½ cups whipping cream

½ cup milk

10 egg yolks

1 tablespoon sugar

½ cup shredded coconut, plus more for garnishing

½ cup canned sweetened coconut cream

5 ounces unsalted macadamia nuts

FOR THE GLAZE

8 1-ounce squares bittersweet chocolate

6 tablespoons butter

1 generous tablespoon light corn syrup

¾ cup whipping cream

1 ▲ Line the bottom and sides of a 6-cup terrine mold (10 × 4 inches) with plastic wrap or wax paper.

2 ▲ Combine the white chocolate and ¼ cup of the cream in the top of a double boiler or in a heatproof bowl set over hot water. Stir until melted and smooth. Set aside.

3 Put 1 cup of the cream and the milk in a heavy saucepan and scald over medium heat.

4 ▲ Meanwhile, in a large bowl, beat the egg yolks and sugar together until thick and pale.

5 ▲ Add the hot cream mixture to the yolks, beating constantly. Pour back into the saucepan and cook over low heat until thickened, 2–3 minutes. Stir constantly and do not boil. Remove from the heat.

6 Stir in the melted chocolate, shredded coconut, and coconut cream until blended. Let cool.

7 Whip the remaining cream until thick. Fold into the chocolate and coconut mixture.

8 Put 2 cups of the parfait mixture in the prepared mold and spread evenly. Cover and freeze until just firm, about 2 hours. Cover the remaining mixture and refrigerate.

9 ▲ Arrange the macadamia nuts evenly over the frozen parfait layer. Pour in the remaining parfait mixture. Cover the mold and freeze until the parfait is firm, 6–8 hours or overnight.

10 ▲ For the glaze, combine the bittersweet chocolate, butter, and corn syrup in the top of a double boiler and stir occasionally until melted.

11 In a saucepan, heat the cream until just simmering. Stir into the chocolate mixture. Remove from the heat and let cool to lukewarm.

12 To unmold the parfait, wrap the mold in a hot towel and set it upside down on a plate. Peel off the plastic wrap or wax paper. Set the parfait on a rack over a baking sheet. Pour the glaze evenly over the top. Working quickly, smooth the glaze down the sides with a metal spatula. Let set slightly, then sprinkle with shredded coconut. Freeze 3–4 hours more.

13 To serve the parfait, slice it with a knife dipped in hot water.

Lemon Pound Cake

SERVES 8–10

1¼ cups (2½ sticks) unsalted butter, at room temperature

1¾ cups granulated sugar

6 eggs

grated rind and juice of 1 large lemon

2⅓ cups sifted cake flour

½ teaspoon salt

confectioners' sugar, for dusting

1 Preheat the oven to 350°F. Grease a 9-cup bundt pan.

2 Beat the butter until it is soft and creamy. Gradually add the sugar and continue beating until fluffy.

3 ▼ Beat in the eggs, one at a time, beating well after each addition. Beat in the lemon rind and juice. Fold in the flour and salt in 3 batches.

4 Pour the batter into the prepared pan and smooth the surface.

5 ▲ Bake until a cake tester inserted in the center comes out clean, 40–50 minutes. Let cool 10 minutes before unmolding onto a wire rack.

6 When the cake is cold, dust it with confectioners' sugar.

Piña Colada Fruit Salad

SERVES 4

1 large pineapple

2 kiwi fruits

¼ cup slivered fresh coconut

2 tablespoons fresh lime juice

1 teaspoon sugar

1–2 tablespoons rum

8 large strawberries, halved

2 ▼ Using a sharp spoon or a grapefruit knife, scoop out the flesh, taking care not to puncture the skin. Cut out and discard the core. Set the pineapple boat aside.

3 Chop the scooped-out flesh into bite-size pieces, keeping any juice, and place in a bowl.

4 Peel the kiwis and chop into bite-size pieces. Add the kiwis and coconut to the pineapple pieces.

5 ▲ In a small bowl, combine the lime juice, sugar, and rum to taste. Stir to blend, then pour over the fruit. Toss well. Cover and refrigerate the fruit salad 1 hour.

6 To serve, spoon the fruit mixture into the pineapple boat. Garnish with the strawberries and serve immediately.

1 ▲ Cut a thick slice off one long side of the pineapple, not cutting into the crown of leaves.

Lemon Pound Cake (top), Pina Colada Fruit Salad

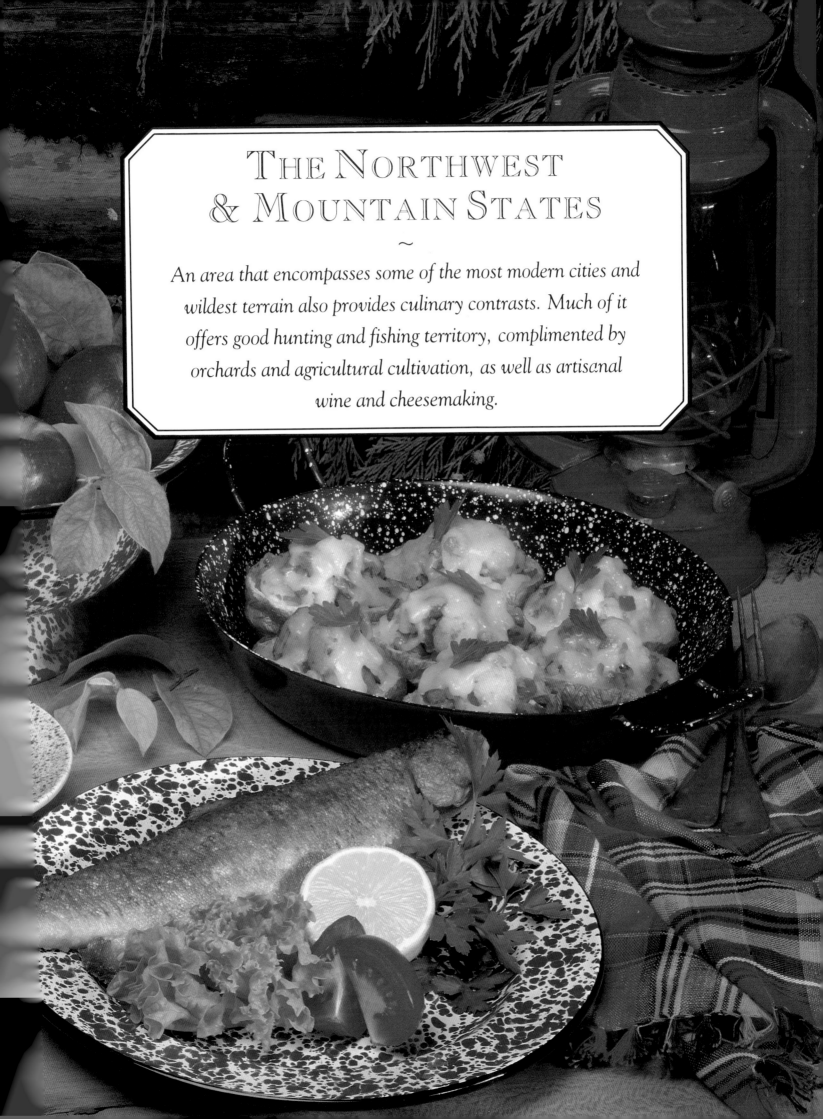

THE NORTHWEST & MOUNTAIN STATES

~

An area that encompasses some of the most modern cities and wildest terrain also provides culinary contrasts. Much of it offers good hunting and fishing territory, complimented by orchards and agricultural cultivation, as well as artisanal wine and cheesemaking.

Salmon Chowder

SERVES 4

1½ tablespoons butter or margarine
1 onion, minced
1 leek, minced
½ cup minced bulb fennel
¼ cup flour
1½ quarts fish stock
2 cups potatoes, cut in ½-inch cubes (about 2 medium-size potatoes)
salt and pepper
1 pound boneless, skinless salmon, cut in ¾-inch cubes
¾ cup milk
½ cup whipping cream
2 tablespoons chopped fresh dill

1 ▲ Melt the butter or margarine in a large saucepan. Add the onion, leek, and fennel and cook over medium heat until softened, 5–8 minutes, stirring occasionally.

2 Stir in the flour. Reduce the heat to low and cook, stirring occasionally, 3 minutes.

3 ▲ Add the stock and potatoes. Season with salt and pepper. Bring to a boil, then reduce the heat, cover, and simmer until the potatoes are tender, about 20 minutes.

4 ▲ Add the salmon and simmer until just cooked, 3–5 minutes.

5 ▲ Stir in the milk, cream, and dill. Cook just until warmed through; do not boil. Taste and adjust the seasoning, if necessary, then serve.

Smoked Turkey and Lentil Soup

SERVES 4

2 tablespoons butter

1 large carrot, chopped

1 onion, chopped

1 celery stalk, chopped

1 leek, white part only, chopped

4 ounces mushrooms, chopped

¼ cup dry white wine

4½ cups chicken stock

2 teaspoons dried thyme

1 bay leaf

½ cup lentils

8 ounces smoked turkey meat, diced

salt and pepper

chopped fresh parsley, for garnishing

1 ▲ Melt the butter in a large saucepan. Add the carrot, onion, leek, celery, and mushrooms. Cook until golden, 3–5 minutes.

2 ▲ Stir in the wine and chicken stock. Bring to a boil and skim any foam that rises to the surface. Add the thyme and bay leaf. Lower the heat, cover, and simmer gently 30 minutes.

3 ▼ Add the lentils and continue cooking, covered, until they are just tender, 30–40 minutes more. Stir the soup from time to time.

4 ▲ Stir in the turkey and season to taste with salt and pepper. Cook until just heated through. Ladle into bowls and garnish with parsley.

Tomato-Blue Cheese Soup with Bacon

SERVES 4

3 pounds ripe tomatoes, peeled,
  quartered, and seeded

2 garlic cloves, minced

salt and pepper

2 tablespoons vegetable oil or butter

1 leek, chopped

1 carrot, chopped

1 quart unsalted chicken stock

4 ounces Oregon Blue cheese, crumbled

3 tablespoons whipping cream

several large fresh basil leaves, or 1–2
  fresh parsley sprigs

6 ounces bacon, cooked and crumbled

1 Preheat the oven to 400°F.

2 ▲ Spread the tomatoes in a baking dish. Sprinkle with the garlic and some salt and pepper. Place in the oven and bake 35 minutes.

3 ▲ Heat the oil or butter in a large saucepan. Add the leek and carrot and season lightly with salt and pepper. Cook over low heat, stirring often, until softened, about 10 minutes.

4 ▲ Stir in the stock and tomatoes. Bring to a boil, then lower the heat, cover, and simmer 20 minutes.

5 ▲ Add the blue cheese, cream, and basil or parsley. Transfer to a food processor or blender and process until smooth (work in batches if necessary). Taste for seasoning.

6 If necessary, reheat the soup, but do not boil. Ladle into bowls and sprinkle with crumbled bacon.

Macaroni and Blue Cheese

SERVES 6

1 pound macaroni

1 quart milk

4 tablespoons butter

6 tablespoons flour

¼ teaspoon salt

8 ounces Oregon Blue cheese, crumbled

black pepper, for serving

1 Preheat the oven to 350°F. Grease a 13- × 9-inch baking dish.

2 ▲ Bring a large pot of water to a boil. Salt to taste and add the macaroni. Cook until just tender (check package directions for cooking times). Drain and rinse under cold water. Place in a large bowl. Set aside.

3 In another pan, bring the milk to a boil and set aside.

4 ▲ Melt the butter in a heavy saucepan over low heat. Whisk in the flour and cook 5 minutes, whisking constantly; do not let the mixture become brown.

5 ▼ Remove from the heat and whisk the hot milk into the butter and flour mixture. When the mixture is smoothly blended, return to medium heat and continue cooking, whisking constantly, until the sauce is thick, about 5 minutes. Add the salt.

6 Add the sauce to the macaroni. Add three-quarters of the crumbled blue cheese and stir well. Transfer the macaroni mixture to the prepared baking dish and spread in an even layer.

7 Sprinkle the remaining cheese evenly over the surface. Bake until bubbling hot, about 25 minutes.

8 If desired, lightly brown the top of the macaroni and cheese under the broiler, 3–4 minutes. Serve hot, sprinkled with freshly ground black pepper.

Smoked Trout Pasta Salad

SERVES 6

1 tablespoon butter

1 cup minced bulb fennel

6 scallions, 2 minced and 4 thinly sliced

salt and pepper

8 ounces skinless smoked trout fillets, flaked

3 tablespoons chopped fresh dill

½ cup mayonnaise

2 teaspoons fresh lemon juice

2 tablespoons whipping cream

1 pound small pasta shapes, such as shells

fresh dill sprigs, for garnishing

1 ▼ Melt the butter in a small nonstick skillet. Add the fennel and minced scallions and season lightly with salt and pepper. Cook over medium heat until just softened, 3–5 minutes. Transfer to a large bowl and let cool slightly.

2 ▲ Add the sliced scallions, trout, dill, mayonnaise, lemon juice, and cream. Mix gently until well blended.

3 ▲ Bring a large pot of water to a boil. Salt to taste and add the pasta. Cook until just tender (check package directions for cooking times). Drain thoroughly and let cool.

4 ▲ Add the pasta to the vegetable and trout mixture and toss to coat evenly. Taste for seasoning. Serve the salad lightly chilled or at room temperature, garnished with dill, if desired.

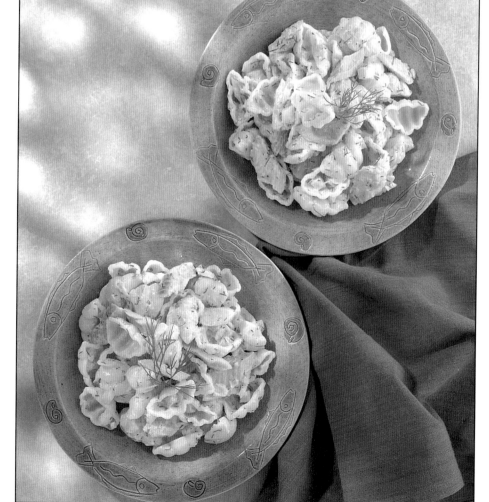

Trout and Bacon Hash

SERVES 2

3 cups potatoes, cut in ½-inch cubes
   (3–4 medium-size potatoes)

salt and pepper

3 tablespoons unsalted butter

½ onion, minced

½ green bell pepper, seeded and minced

1 garlic clove, minced

2 ounces Canadian bacon, chopped

7 ounces skinless trout fillets, cut in
   ½-inch pieces

1 teaspoon dried oregano

1 tablespoon chopped fresh parsley
   (optional)

3 ▼ Add the remaining butter and the potatoes to the skillet. Cook over high heat, stirring occasionally, until the potatoes are lightly browned, about 5 minutes longer.

4 ▲ Add the trout, oregano, and parsley if using. Season with salt and pepper. Continue cooking, smashing down with a wooden spatula, until the trout is cooked through, 3–4 minutes more. Serve immediately.

1 ▲ Put the potatoes in a saucepan, add cold water to cover, and bring to a boil. Add 1 tablespoon salt and simmer until just tender, 8–10 minutes. Drain and set aside.

2 ▲ Melt 2 tablespoons of the butter in a large nonstick skillet. Add the onion, bell pepper, garlic, and bacon and cook over medium heat until the onion is just softened, 5–8 minutes.

Seattle Fish Fritters

SERVES 4

½ fennel bulb, cut in pieces

1 medium leek, cut in pieces

1 green bell pepper, seeded and cut in pieces

2 garlic cloves

1 tablespoon butter

⅛ teaspoon red pepper flakes

salt and pepper

6 ounces skinless boneless salmon, cut in pieces

3½ ounces skinless boneless rockfish or ling cod, cut in pieces

3 ounces cooked peeled shrimp

1 cup flour

6 eggs, beaten

1½–2 cups milk

1 tablespoon chopped fresh basil

4–6 tablespoons oil, for greasing

sour cream, for serving

1 ▲ Combine the fennel, leek, bell pepper, and garlic in a food processor and process until finely chopped.

~ VARIATION ~

For Seattle Salmon Fritters, increase the amount of salmon to ¾ pound, and omit the rockfish or ling cod and shrimp. Use dill in place of the basil. Serve with a tossed green salad, if desired.

2 ▲ Melt the butter in a skillet until sizzling. Add the vegetable mixture and red pepper flakes. Season with salt and pepper. Cook over low heat until softened, 8–10 minutes. Remove from the heat and set aside.

3 ▲ Combine the salmon, rockfish or ling cod, and shrimp in the food processor. Process, using the pulse button and scraping the sides of the container several times, until the mixture is coarsely chopped. Scrape into a large bowl and set aside.

4 ▲ Sift the flour into another bowl and make a well in the center.

5 ▲ Gradually whisk in the eggs alternately with 1½ cups milk to make a smooth batter. If necessary, strain the batter to remove lumps.

6 ▲ Stir the seafood, vegetables, and basil into the batter. If it seems too thick, add a little more milk.

7 ▲ Lightly oil a griddle or nonstick skillet and heat over medium heat. Spoon in the batter by ⅓-cupfuls. Cook until the fritters are golden around the edges, 2–3 minutes. Turn them over and cook the other side, 2–3 minutes more. Work in batches, keeping the cooked fritters warm.

8 Serve hot, with sour cream.

Scalloped Oysters

SERVES 4

7 tablespoons butter
1 shallot, minced
4 ounces mushrooms, minced
½ teaspoon flour
⅛ teaspoon hot pepper sauce
salt and pepper
24 oysters, shucked and drained
⅓ cup dry white wine
⅔ cup whipping cream
2 tablespoons chopped fresh parsley
6 tablespoons fresh bread crumbs

1 Preheat the oven to 375°F. Grease a 6- × 8-inch baking dish.

2 Melt the butter in a large skillet. Add the shallot and mushrooms and cook until softened, about 3 minutes.

3 ▼ Add the flour and hot pepper sauce. Season with salt and pepper. Cook, stirring constantly, 1 minute.

4 ▲ Stir in the oysters and wine, scraping the bottom of the skillet. Add the cream. Transfer the mixture to the prepared baking dish.

5 ▲ In a small bowl, combine the chopped parsley, fresh bread crumbs, and salt to taste. Stir to mix.

6 ▲ Sprinkle the crumbs evenly over the oyster mixture. Bake until the top is golden and the sauce bubbling, 15–20 minutes. Serve immediately.

Penn Cove Steamed Mussels

SERVES 2

1½ pounds mussels in shell
½ fennel bulb, minced
1 shallot, minced
3 tablespoons dry white wine
3 tablespoons whipping cream
2 tablespoons chopped fresh parsley
black pepper

1 ▲ Scrub the mussels under cold running water. Remove any barnacles with a small knife, and remove the beards. Rinse once more.

2 ▲ Place the mussels in a large skillet with a lid. Sprinkle them with the fennel, shallot, and wine. Cover the skillet and place over medium-high heat. Steam until the mussels open, 3–5 minutes.

3 Lift out the mussels with a slotted spoon and remove the top shells. Discard any mussels that did not open. Arrange the mussels, on their bottom shells, in one layer in a shallow serving dish. Keep warm.

4 ▼ Place a double layer of dampened cheesecloth in a strainer set over a bowl. Strain the mussel cooking liquid through the cheesecloth. Return the liquid to a clean saucepan and bring to a boil.

5 ▲ Add the cream, stir well, and boil 3 minutes to reduce slightly. Stir in the parsley. Spoon the sauce over the mussels and sprinkle with freshly ground black pepper. Serve the mussels immediately.

Stuffed Potato Skins

SERVES 6

3 baking potatoes, about 12 ounces each, scrubbed and patted dry
1 tablespoon vegetable oil
3 tablespoons butter
1 onion, chopped
salt and pepper
1 green bell pepper, seeded and coarsely chopped
1 teaspoon paprika
1 cup shredded Monterey Jack or cheddar cheese

1 Preheat the oven to 450°F.

2 ▲ Brush the potatoes all over with the oil. Prick them in several places on all sides with a fork.

3 ▲ Place in a baking dish. Bake until tender, about 1½ hours.

4 ▲ Meanwhile, heat the butter in a large nonstick skillet. Add the onion and a little salt and cook over medium heat until softened, about 5 minutes. Add the bell pepper and continue cooking until just tender but still crunchy, 2–3 minutes more. Stir in the paprika and set aside.

5 ▲ When the potatoes are done, halve them lengthwise. Scoop out the flesh, keeping the pieces coarse. Keep the potato skins warm.

6 Preheat the broiler.

> **~ VARIATION ~**
>
> For Bacon-Stuffed Potato Skins, add ¾ cup chopped cooked bacon to the cooked potato flesh and vegetables. Stuff as above.

7 ▲ Add the potato flesh to the skillet and cook over high heat, stirring, until the potato is lightly browned. Season with pepper.

8 ▲ Divide the vegetable mixture among the potato skins.

9 ▲ Sprinkle the cheese on top. Broil until the cheese just melts, 3–5 minutes. Serve immediately.

Pasta with Scallops

SERVES 4

1 pound pasta, such as fettucine or linguine

2 tablespoons olive oil

2 garlic cloves, minced

1 pound sea scallops, sliced in half horizontally

salt and pepper

FOR THE SAUCE

2 tablespoons olive oil

½ onion, minced

1 garlic clove, minced

½ teaspoon salt

1 28-ounce can peeled tomatoes

2 tablespoons chopped fresh basil

1 For the sauce, heat the oil in a nonstick skillet. Add the onion, garlic, and a little salt, and cook over medium heat until just softened, about 5 minutes, stirring occasionally.

2 ▲ Add the tomatoes, with their juice, and crush with the tines of a fork. Bring to a boil, then reduce the heat and simmer gently 15 minutes. Remove from the heat and set aside.

3 ▲ Bring a large pot of salted water to a boil. Add the pasta and cook until just tender to the bite (check package directions for timing).

4 ▲ Meanwhile, combine the oil and garlic in another nonstick skillet and cook until just sizzling, about 30 seconds. Add the scallops and ½ teaspoon salt and cook over high heat, tossing, until the scallops are cooked through, about 3 minutes.

5 ▲ Add the scallops to the tomato sauce. Season with salt and pepper, stir, and keep warm.

6 Drain the pasta, rinse under hot water, and drain again. Place in a large warmed serving bowl. Add the scallop sauce and the basil and toss thoroughly. Serve immediately.

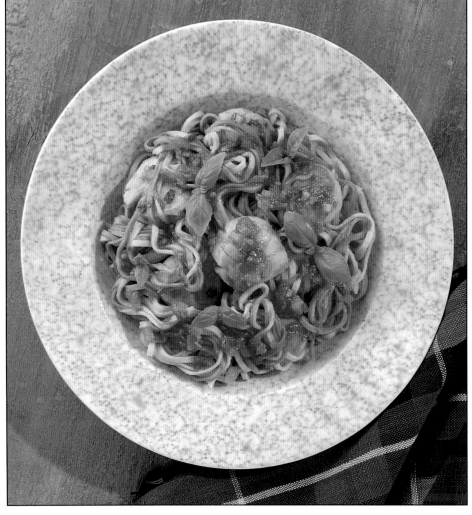

Clam and Sausage Chili

SERVES 4

1 cup dried black beans, soaked overnight and drained
1 bay leaf
2 teaspoons coarse salt
½ pound lean bulk pork sausage meat
1 tablespoon vegetable oil
1 onion, minced
1 garlic clove, minced
1 teaspoon fennel seeds
1 teaspoon dried oregano
¼ teaspoon red pepper flakes, or to taste
2–3 teaspoons chili powder, or to taste
1 teaspoon ground cumin
2 16-ounce cans chopped tomatoes in purée
½ cup dry white wine
1½ cups drained canned clams (approximately 2 10-ounce cans), liquid reserved
salt and pepper

1 Put the beans in a large pot. Add fresh cold water to cover and the bay leaf. Bring to a boil, then cover, and simmer 30 minutes. Add the coarse salt and continue simmering until tender, about 30 minutes more. Drain and discard the bay leaf.

2 ▲ Put the sausage meat in a large flameproof casserole. Cook over medium heat until just beginning to brown, 2–3 minutes. Stir frequently to break up lumps. Add the oil, onion, and garlic.

3 Continue cooking until the vegetables are softened, about 5 minutes more, stirring occasionally.

4 ▼ Stir in the herbs and spices, tomatoes, wine, and ⅔ cup of the reserved clam juice. Bring to a boil, then lower the heat and cook, stirring occasionally, 15 minutes.

5 ▲ Add the black beans and clams and stir to combine. Taste and adjust the seasoning if necessary. Continue cooking just until the clams are heated through. Serve immediately.

Pan-Fried Trout with Horseradish Sauce

SERVES 4

4 whole rainbow trout, about 6 ounces each, cleaned
salt and pepper
¼ cup flour
2 tablespoons butter
1 tablespoon vegetable oil
FOR THE SAUCE
½ cup mayonnaise
½ cup sour cream
¾ teaspoon grated horseradish
¼ teaspoon paprika
2 tablespoons tomato or lemon juice
1 tablespoon chopped fresh herbs, such as chives, parsley, or basil

1 ▼ For the sauce, combine the mayonnaise, sour cream, horseradish, paprika, tomato or lemon juice, and herbs. Season with salt and pepper and mix well. Set the sauce aside.

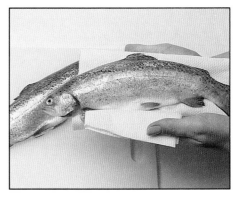

2 ▲ Rinse the trout and pat dry. Season the cavities in the fish generously with salt and pepper.

3 ▲ Combine the flour, ½ teaspoon salt, and a little pepper in a shallow dish. Coat the trout on both sides with the seasoned flour, shaking off any excess.

4 ▲ Heat the butter and oil in a large nonstick skillet over medium-high heat. When sizzling, add the trout and cook until opaque throughout, 4–5 minutes on each side. Serve immediately, with the sauce.

Salmon with Sizzling Herbs

SERVES 4

4 salmon steaks, 6–7 ounces each

salt and pepper

⅓ cup olive oil

½ cup chopped fresh coriander (cilantro)

3 tablespoons minced fresh gingerroot

½ cup chopped scallions

¼ cup soy sauce, plus extra for serving

1 Bring some water to a boil in the bottom of a steamer.

2 ▲ Season the fish steaks on both sides with salt and pepper.

3 ▲ Place the fish steaks in the top part of the steamer. Cover the pan and steam until the fish is opaque throughout, 7–8 minutes.

4 ▼ Meanwhile, heat the oil in a small heavy saucepan until very hot. (To test the temperature, drop in a piece of chopped scallion; if it sizzles, the oil is hot enough.)

5 Place the steamed salmon steaks on warmed plates.

6 ▲ Divide the chopped coriander among the salmon steaks, mounding it on top of the fish. Sprinkle with the ginger and then the scallions. Drizzle 1 tablespoon of soy sauce over each salmon steak.

7 Spoon the hot oil over each salmon steak and serve immediately, with additional soy sauce.

Pork Chops with Cider and Apples

SERVES 4

1 pound tart cooking apples (3–4), peeled, quartered, and cored
4 pork chops, about 1 inch thick
1 teaspoon dried thyme
¼ teaspoon ground allspice
salt and pepper
1 tablespoon butter
1 tablespoon vegetable oil
1 bay leaf
½ cup apple cider
2 tablespoons whipping cream
potato pancakes, for serving

1 Preheat the oven to 375°F. Grease a casserole large enough to hold the pork chops in one layer.

2 ▲ Spread the apples in an even layer in the prepared dish. Set aside.

3 Sprinkle the pork chops on both sides with the thyme, ground allspice, and a little salt and pepper.

4 Heat the butter and oil in a skillet. When hot, add the pork chops and cook over medium-high heat until browned, 2–3 minutes. Turn and cook the other side, 2–3 minutes more. Remove from the heat.

5 ▲ Arrange the pork chops on top of the apples. Add the bay leaf and pour over the cider. Cover and bake for 15 minutes.

6 ▲ Turn the chops over. Continue baking until they are cooked through, about 15 minutes more.

7 Transfer the pork chops to warmed plates. Remove the apple quarters with a slotted spoon and divide them equally among the plates.

8 Stir the cream into the sauce and heat just until warmed through. Taste for seasoning. Spoon the sauce over the pork chops and serve immediately, with potato pancakes.

Pork Braised in Beer

SERVES 6

4–5-pound loin of pork, boned, trimmed of excess fat, and tied into a neat shape
salt and pepper
1 tablespoon butter
1 tablespoon vegetable oil
3 large onions, halved and thinly sliced
1 garlic clove, minced
3 cups beer
1 bay leaf
1 tablespoon flour blended with 2 tablespoons water

1 ▲ Season the pork roast on all sides with salt and pepper. Heat the butter and oil in a flameproof casserole just large enough to hold the pork loin. When hot, add the roast and brown on all sides, 5–7 minutes, turning it to color evenly. Remove from the pot and set aside.

2 ▲ Drain excess fat from the pot, leaving about 1 tablespoon. Add the onions and garlic and cook just until softened, about 5 minutes.

3 ▲ Stir in the beer, scraping to remove any bits on the bottom of the pan. Add the bay leaf.

4 Return the pork roast to the casserole. Cover and cook over low heat about 2 hours, turning the roast halfway through the cooking time.

5 ▼ Remove the pork roast. Cut it into serving slices and arrange on a platter. Cover and keep warm.

6 Discard the bay leaf. Add the flour to the cooking juices and cook over high heat, stirring constantly, until thickened. Taste for seasoning. Pour the sauce over the pork slices and serve immediately.

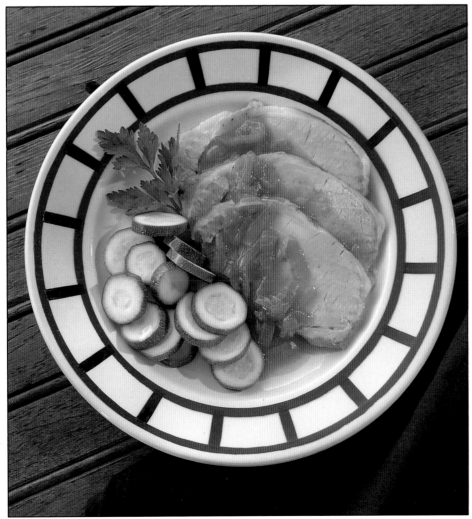

Chicken-Mushroom Pie

SERVES 6

½ ounce dried porcini mushrooms

4 tablespoons butter

2 tablespoons flour

1 cup chicken stock, warmed

¼ cup whipping cream or milk

salt and pepper

1 onion, coarsely chopped

2 carrots, sliced

2 celery stalks, coarsely chopped

2 ounces fresh mushrooms, quartered

1 pound cooked chicken meat, cubed

½ cup shelled fresh or frozen peas

beaten egg, for glazing

FOR THE CRUST

2 cups flour

¼ teaspoon salt

½ cup (1 stick) cold butter, cut in pieces

⅓ cup shortening

4–8 tablespoons ice water

1 ▲ For the crust, sift the flour and salt into a bowl. With a pastry blender or 2 knives, cut in the butter and shortening until the mixture resembles coarse meal. Sprinkle with 6 tablespoons ice water and mix until the dough holds together. If the dough is too crumbly, add a little more water, 1 tablespoon at a time. Gather the dough into a ball and flatten into a disk. Wrap in wax paper and refrigerate at least 30 minutes.

2 Place the porcini mushrooms in a small bowl. Add hot water to cover and soak until soft, about 30 minutes. Lift out of the water with a slotted spoon to leave any grit behind and drain. Discard the soaking water.

3 Preheat the oven to 375°F.

4 ▲ Melt 2 tablespoons of the butter in a heavy saucepan. Whisk in the flour and cook until bubbling, whisking constantly. Add the warm stock and cook over medium heat, whisking, until the mixture boils. Cook 2–3 minutes more. Whisk in the cream or milk. Season with salt and pepper. Set aside.

5 ▲ Heat the remaining butter in a large nonstick skillet until foamy. Add the onion and carrots and cook until softened, about 5 minutes. Add the celery and fresh mushrooms and cook 5 minutes more. Stir in the chicken, peas, and drained porcini mushrooms.

6 Add the chicken mixture to the cream sauce and stir to mix. Taste for seasoning. Transfer to a 10-cup rectangular baking dish.

7 ▲ Roll out the dough to about ⅛-inch thickness. Cut out a rectangle about 1 inch larger all around than the dish. Lay the rectangle of dough over the filling. Make a decorative edge, crimping the dough by pushing the index finger of one hand between the thumb and index finger of the other.

8 Cut several vents in the top crust to allow steam to escape. Brush with the egg glaze.

9 ▲ Press together the dough trimmings, then roll out again. Cut into strips and lay them over the top crust. Glaze again. If desired, roll small balls of dough and set them in the "windows" in the lattice.

10 Bake until the top crust is browned, about 30 minutes. Serve the pie hot from the dish.

Oregon Blue Cheese Burgers

SERVES 4

2 pounds lean ground beef

1 garlic clove, minced

2 tablespoons chopped fresh parsley

2 tablespoons chopped fresh chives

½ teaspoon salt

pepper

8 ounces Oregon Blue cheese, crumbled

4 hamburger buns, split and toasted

tomato slices and lettuce, for serving

mustard or catsup, for serving

1 ▼ In a bowl, combine the beef, garlic, parsley, chives, salt, and a little pepper. Mix lightly together, then form into 4 thick patties.

2 ▲ Make a slit in the side of each patty, poking well into the beef to form a pocket. Fill each pocket with 2 ounces of the blue cheese.

3 ▲ Close the holes to seal the blue cheese inside the patties.

4 Heat a ridged grill pan (or preheat the broiler).

5 Cook the burgers 4–5 minutes on each side for medium-rare, 6–7 minutes for well-done.

6 ▲ Place the burgers in the split hamburger buns. Serve immediately, with sliced tomatoes and lettuce leaves, and mustard or catsup if desired.

Steak with Mushrooms and Leeks in Red Wine

SERVES 4

6–8 leeks (about 1¼ pounds), white and light green parts only

¼ cup olive oil

1½ pounds mushrooms, quartered

2 cups dry red wine, such as an Oregon Pinot Noir or a Washington State Merlot

salt and pepper

4 8-ounce boneless sirloin steaks, about ¾ inch thick

1 tablespoon chopped fresh parsley

1 ▲ Trim the leeks and cut into 1-inch slices on the diagonal.

2 ▲ Heat 3 tablespoons of the oil in a large skillet. When hot, add the leeks and mushrooms and cook over medium heat, stirring often, until lightly browned.

3 Stir in the wine, scraping the bottom of the pan. Season with salt and pepper. Bring to a boil and boil 1 minute. Reduce the heat to low, then cover and cook 5 minutes.

4 Remove the lid, raise the heat, and cook until the wine has reduced slightly, about 5 minutes. Set aside.

5 ▼ Brush the steaks with the remaining 1 tablespoon oil and sprinkle generously on both sides with salt and pepper.

6 Heat a ridged grill pan (or preheat the broiler). When hot, add the steaks and cook 3–4 minutes on each side for medium-rare.

7 Meanwhile, stir the parsley into the leek mixture and reheat.

8 Place the steaks on 4 warmed plates. Mound the leek mixture on top and serve.

~ **VARIATION** ~

If available, use fresh wild mushrooms for extra flavor.

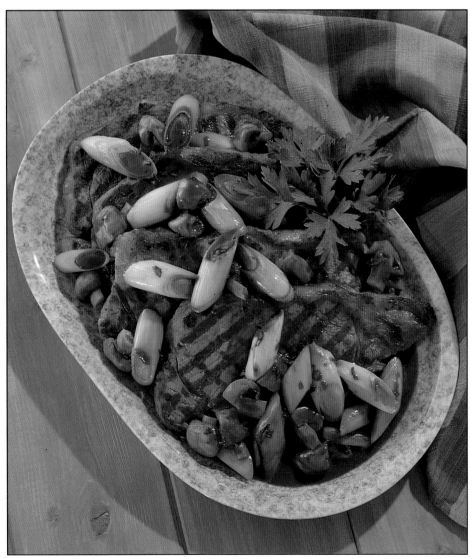

Idaho Beef Stew

SERVES 6

¼ cup vegetable oil
2 onions, chopped
4 large carrots, thickly sliced
3 pounds chuck steak, cubed
salt and pepper
3 tablespoons flour
3 cups unsalted beef stock
1 cup strong black coffee
2 teaspoons dried oregano
1 bay leaf
1 cup shelled fresh or frozen peas
mashed potatoes, for serving

1 ▼ Heat 2 tablespoons of the oil in a large flameproof casserole. Add the onions and carrots and cook over medium heat until lightly browned, about 8 minutes. Remove them with a slotted spoon, transfer to a plate or dish, and reserve.

2 ▲ Add another tablespoon of oil to the casserole and then add the beef cubes. Raise the heat to medium-high and cook until browned all over. (Work in batches if necessary.) Season with salt and pepper.

3 ▲ Return the vegetables to the casserole. Add the flour and the remaining tablespoon of oil. Cook, stirring constantly, 1 minute. Add the stock, coffee, oregano, and bay leaf. Bring to a boil and cook, stirring often, until thickened. Reduce the heat to low, then cover the casserole and simmer gently until the beef is tender, about 45 minutes.

4 ▲ Add the peas and simmer 5–10 minutes more. Discard the bay leaf, and taste for seasoning. Serve hot, with mashed potatoes.

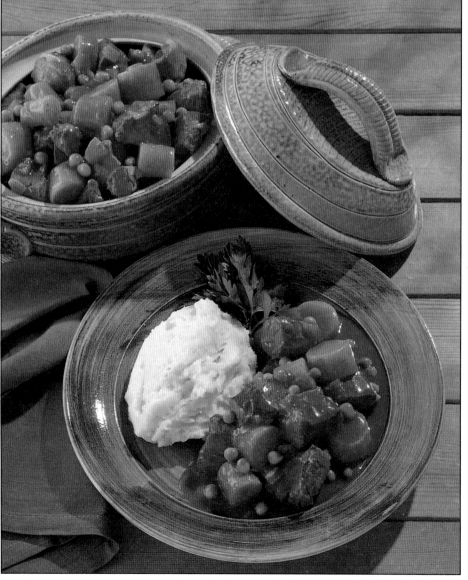

Pot-Roasted Veal Chops with Carrots

SERVES 4

1 tablespoon vegetable oil
1 tablespoon butter
4 veal chops, about ¾ inch thick
salt and pepper
1 onion, halved and thinly sliced
½ cup dry white wine
1½ pounds carrots, cut in ½-inch slices
1 bay leaf
½ cup whipping cream

1 Preheat the oven to 350°F.

2 ▲ Heat the oil and butter in a flameproof casserole large enough to hold the veal chops in one layer. Add the chops and cook over medium heat until well browned on both sides, 6–8 minutes. Transfer to a plate, season with salt and pepper, and set aside.

3 ▲ Add the onion to the pot and cook until it is just softened, about 5 minutes. Stir in the wine.

4 ▼ Return the veal chops to the pot. Add the carrots. Season with salt and pepper and add the bay leaf.

5 Cover the casserole and transfer it to the oven. Cook until the chops are tender, about 30 minutes.

6 Remove the chops and carrots to warm plates and keep warm. Discard the bay leaf. Stir the cream into the cooking liquid and bring to a boil. Simmer until the sauce is slightly thickened, 2–3 minutes.

7 Taste the sauce and adjust the seasoning if necessary, then spoon it over the chops. Serve immediately.

Cauliflower au Gratin

SERVES 4

2½ pounds cauliflower florets (about 1 large head)

3 tablespoons butter

3 tablespoons flour

2 cups milk

½ cup shredded sharp cheddar cheese

salt and pepper

3 bay leaves

1 ▲ Preheat the oven to 350°F. Grease a 12-inch round baking dish.

2 Bring a large pot of salted water to a boil. Add the cauliflower and cook until just tender but still firm, 7–8 minutes. Drain well.

3 ▲ Melt the butter in a heavy saucepan. Whisk in the flour until thoroughly blended and cook until bubbling. Gradually add the milk. Bring to a boil and continue cooking, stirring constantly, until thick.

4 ▲ Remove from the heat and stir in the shredded cheese. Season the sauce with salt and pepper.

5 ▲ Place the bay leaves on the bottom of the prepared dish. Arrange the cauliflower florets on top in an even layer. Pour the cheese sauce evenly over the cauliflower.

6 Bake until browned, 20–25 minutes. Serve immediately.

Wild Rice Pilaf

SERVES 6

1 cup wild rice

salt and pepper

3 tablespoons butter

½ onion, minced

1 cup long-grain rice

2 cups chicken stock

⅔ cup sliced or slivered almonds

⅔ cup golden raisins

2 tablespoons chopped fresh parsley

3 Stir in the stock and bring to a boil. Cover and simmer gently until the rice is tender and the liquid has been absorbed, 30–40 minutes.

4 ▼ Melt the remaining butter in a small skillet. Add the almonds and cook until they are just golden, 2–3 minutes, stirring. Set aside.

5 ▲ In a large bowl, combine the wild rice, long-grain rice, raisins, almonds, and parsley. Stir to mix. Taste and adjust the seasoning if necessary. Transfer to a warmed serving dish and serve immediately.

1 ▲ Bring a large saucepan of water to a boil. Add the wild rice and 1 teaspoon salt. Cover and simmer gently until the rice is tender, 45–60 minutes. When done, drain well.

2 ▲ Meanwhile, melt 1 tablespoon of the butter in another saucepan. Add the onion and cook over medium heat until it is just softened, about 5 minutes. Stir in the long-grain rice and cook 1 minute more.

Blue Cheese-Chive Pennies

MAKES 4 DOZEN

8 ounces Oregon Blue cheese, crumbled

½ cup (1 stick) unsalted butter, at room
    temperature

1 egg

1 egg yolk

3 tablespoons chopped fresh chives

black pepper

2 cups flour, sifted

1 ▼ The day before serving, beat the
cheese and butter together until well
blended. Add the egg, egg yolk,
chives, and a little pepper and beat
just until blended.

2 ▲ Add the flour in 3 batches,
folding in well between each addition.

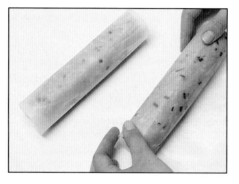

3 ▲ Divide the dough in half and
shape each half into a log about
2 inches in diameter. Wrap in wax
paper and refrigerate overnight.

4 Preheat the oven to 375°F. Lightly
grease 2 baking sheets.

5 ▲ Cut the dough logs across into
slices about ⅛ inch thick. Place on
the prepared sheets.

6 Bake until just golden around the
edges, about 10 minutes. Transfer to a
wire rack to cool.

~ **COOK'S TIP** ~

The cheese pennies will keep up to
10 days in an airtight container.

Dilled Smoked Salmon Spread

MAKES 3 CUPS

1 cup ricotta cheese

1 cup cream cheese, at room
    temperature

6 ounces smoked salmon, finely
    chopped

4 ounces cooked salmon, flaked

¼ cup chopped fresh dill

3–4 tablespoons fresh lemon juice

salt and pepper

vegetables, such as cucumber slices,
    Belgian endive leaves, bell pepper
    strips, or small toasts, for serving

1 ▲ In a food processor or blender,
combine the ricotta cheese, cream
cheese, and smoked salmon. Process
until light and fluffy. Scrape the
mixture into a bowl.

2 ▼ Stir in the cooked salmon, dill,
and 3 tablespoons of the lemon juice.
Season with salt and pepper. Taste
and add the remaining lemon juice if
desired. Serve the spread cold.

Blue Cheese-Chive Pennies (top), Dilled Smoked Salmon Spread

Winter Warmer (Hot White Chocolate)

SERVES 4

6 ounces white chocolate

1½ quarts milk

1 teaspoon coffee extract, or 2 teaspoons instant coffee powder

2 teaspoons orange-flavored liqueur (optional)

FOR SERVING

whipped cream

ground cinnamon

> ~ **COOK'S TIP** ~
>
> If preferred, use milk chocolate or semisweet dark chocolate instead of white chocolate, but taste before serving in case a little sugar is needed.

1 ▼ With a sharp knife, finely chop the white chocolate. (Try not to handle it too much or it will soften and stick together.)

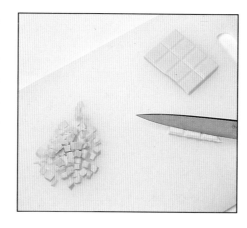

2 Pour the milk into a medium-sized heavy saucepan and bring just to a boil (bubbles will form around the edge of the pan).

3 ▲ Add the chopped white chocolate, coffee extract or powder, and orange-flavored liqueur if using. Stir until the chocolate has melted.

4 Divide the hot chocolate among 4 coffee mugs. Top each with a rosette or spoonful of whipped cream and a sprinkling of ground cinnamon. Serve immediately.

Easy Hazelnut Fudge

MAKES 16 SQUARES

⅔ cup evaporated milk

1¾ cups sugar

⅛ teaspoon salt

½ cup halved hazelnuts

2 cups semisweet chocolate chips

1 teaspoon hazelnut liqueur (optional)

1 Generously grease an 8-inch square cake pan.

> ~ **VARIATION** ~
>
> For Easy Peanut Butter Fudge, substitute peanut butter chips for the chocolate chips and replace the hazelnuts with peanuts.

2 Combine the evaporated milk, sugar, and salt in a heavy saucepan. Bring to a boil over medium heat, stirring constantly. Simmer gently, stirring, about 5 minutes.

3 ▼ Remove from the heat and add the hazelnuts, chocolate chips, and liqueur if using. Stir until the chocolate has completely melted.

4 ▲ Quickly pour the fudge mixture into the prepared pan and spread it out evenly. Let cool.

5 When the fudge is set, cut into 1-inch squares. Store in an airtight container, separating the layers with wax paper.

Winter Warmer (top), Easy Hazelnut Fudge

Northwestern Brown Betty

SERVES 6

2¼ pounds pears (about 8)

¼ cup lemon juice

3 cups fresh bread crumbs, preferably from egg bread

6 tablespoons butter, melted

⅔ cup dried cherries

⅔ cup coarsely chopped hazelnuts

½ cup brown sugar, firmly packed

1–2 tablespoons butter, cut in small pieces

whipped cream, for serving

1 Preheat the oven to 375°F. Grease an 8-inch square cake pan.

2 ▼ Peel, core, and dice the pears. Sprinkle them with the lemon juice to prevent discoloration.

3 ▲ Combine the bread crumbs and melted butter in a bowl. Spread a scant one-third of the crumb mixture on the bottom of the prepared dish.

4 ▲ Top with half of the pears. Sprinkle over half of the dried cherries, half of the hazelnuts, and half of the sugar. Repeat the layers, then finish with a layer of crumbs.

5 ▲ Dot with the pieces of butter. Bake until golden, 30–35 minutes. Serve hot, with whipped cream.

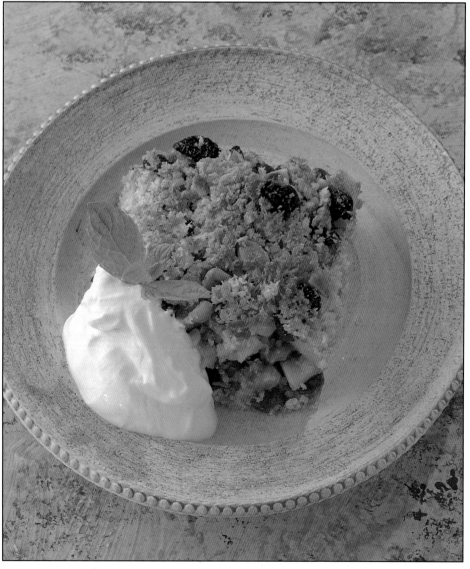

Rhubarb-Strawberry Crisp

SERVES 4

8 ounces strawberries, hulled
1 pound rhubarb, diced
½ cup granulated sugar
1 tablespoon cornstarch
⅓ cup fresh orange juice
1 cup flour
1 cup rolled oats
½ cup light brown sugar, firmly packed
½ teaspoon ground cinnamon
½ cup ground almonds
10 tablespoons (1¼ sticks) cold butter
1 egg, lightly beaten

1 Preheat the oven to 350°F.

2 ▲ If the strawberries are large, cut them in half. Combine the strawberries, rhubarb, and granulated sugar in a 2-quart baking dish.

3 ▲ In a small bowl, blend the cornstarch with the orange juice. Pour this mixture over the fruit and stir gently to coat. Set the baking dish aside while making the topping.

4 ▼ In a bowl, toss together the flour, oats, brown sugar, cinnamon, and almonds. With a pastry blender or 2 knives, cut in the butter until the mixture resembles coarse crumbs. Stir in the beaten egg.

5 ▲ Spoon the oat mixture evenly over the fruit and press down gently. Bake until browned, 50–60 minutes. Serve the crisp warm.

Blackberry Cobbler

Serves 8

6 cups blackberries (about 1¾ pounds)

1 cup sugar

3 tablespoons flour

grated rind of 1 lemon

2 tablespoons sugar mixed with
 ¼ teaspoon grated nutmeg

For the topping

2 cups flour

1 cup sugar

1 tablespoon baking powder

⅛ teaspoon salt

1 cup milk

½ cup (1 stick) butter, melted

1 Preheat the oven to 350°F.

2 ▼ In a bowl, combine the blackberries, sugar, flour, and lemon rind. Stir gently to blend. Transfer to a 2-quart baking dish.

3 ▲ For the topping, sift the flour, sugar, baking powder, and salt into a large bowl. Set aside. In a large measure, combine the milk and butter.

4 ▲ Gradually stir the milk mixture into the dry ingredients and stir until the batter is just smooth.

5 ▲ Spoon the batter over the berries, spreading to the edges.

6 Sprinkle the surface with the sugar-nutmeg mixture. Bake until the batter topping is set and lightly browned, about 50 minutes. Serve hot.

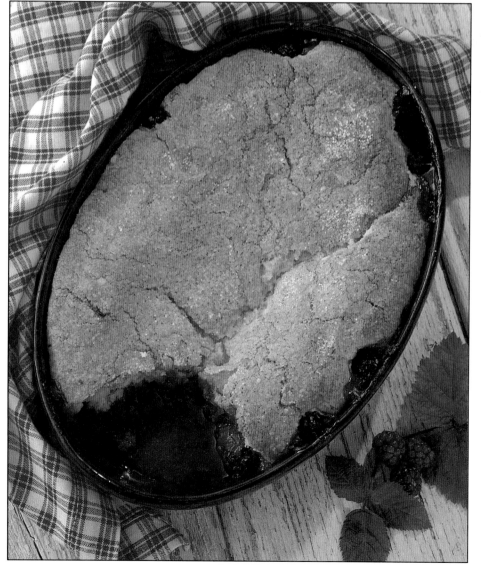

Baked Apples

SERVES 6

½ cup chopped dried apricots

½ cup chopped walnuts

1 teaspoon grated lemon rind

¼ teaspoon ground cinnamon

½ cup light brown sugar, firmly packed

2 tablespoons butter, at room
    temperature

6 baking apples

1 tablespoon melted butter

1 Preheat the oven to 375°F.

2 ▲ In a bowl, combine the apricots, walnuts, lemon rind, and cinnamon. Add the sugar and butter and stir until thoroughly combined.

3 ▲ Core the apples, without cutting all the way through to the base. With a small knife, slightly widen the top of each opening by about 1½ inches to make room for the filling.

4 Spoon the apricot and walnut filling into the opening in the apples, packing it down lightly.

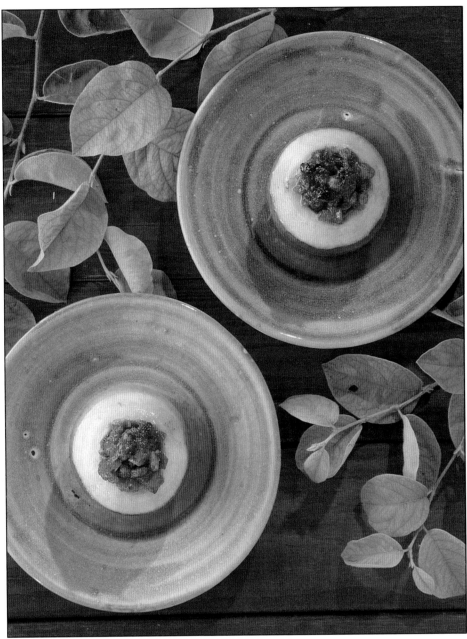

5 ▼ Place the apples in a baking dish just large enough to hold them comfortably side by side.

6 ▲ Brush the apples with the melted butter. Bake until they are tender, 40–45 minutes. Serve hot.

Blueberry-Hazelnut Cheesecake

SERVES 6–8

12 ounces blueberries

1 tablespoon honey

6 tablespoons granulated sugar

1 teaspoon plus 1 tablespoon fresh lemon juice

6 ounces cream cheese, at room temperature

1 egg

1 teaspoon hazelnut liqueur (optional)

½ cup whipping cream

FOR THE CRUST

1⅔ cups ground hazelnuts

⅔ cup flour

⅛ teaspoon salt

4 tablespoons butter, at room temperature

⅓ cup light brown sugar, firmly packed

1 egg yolk

1 ▲ For the crust, put the hazelnuts in a large bowl. Sift in the flour and salt, and stir to mix. Set aside.

~ COOK'S TIP ~

The cheesecake can be prepared 1 day in advance, but add the fruit shortly before serving. Instead of covering the top completely, leave spaces to make a design, if wished.

2 Beat the butter with the brown sugar until light and fluffy. Beat in the egg yolk. Gradually fold in the nut mixture, in 3 batches.

3 ▲ Press the dough into a greased 9-inch pie pan, spreading it evenly against the sides. Form a rim around the top edge that is slightly thicker than the sides. Cover and refrigerate at least 30 minutes.

4 Preheat the oven to 350°F.

5 ▲ Meanwhile, for the topping, combine the blueberries, honey, 1 tablespoon of the granulated sugar, and 1 teaspoon lemon juice in a heavy saucepan. Cook the mixture over low heat, stirring occasionally, until the berries have given off some liquid but still retain their shape, 5–7 minutes. Remove from the heat and set aside.

6 Place the crust in the oven and bake 15 minutes. Remove and let cool while making the filling.

7 ▲ Beat together the cream cheese and remaining granulated sugar until light and fluffy. Add the egg, remaining lemon juice, the liqueur, if using, and the cream and beat until thoroughly incorporated.

8 ▲ Pour the cheese mixture into the crust and spread evenly. Bake until just set, 20–25 minutes.

9 Let the cheesecake cool completely on a wire rack, then cover and refrigerate at least 1 hour.

10 Spread the blueberry mixture evenly over the top of the cheesecake. Serve at cool room temperature.

Chocolate-Coffee-Vanilla Pudding Cups

SERVES 6

1½ cups sugar

6 tablespoons cornstarch

4 cups milk

3 egg yolks

6 tablespoons unsalted butter, at room temperature

1 generous tablespoon instant coffee powder

2 teaspoons vanilla extract

2 tablespoons unsweetened cocoa powder

whipped cream, for serving

1 ▲ For the coffee layer, combine ½ cup of the sugar and 2 tablespoons of the cornstarch in a heavy saucepan. Gradually add 1⅓ cups of the milk, whisking until well blended. Over medium heat, whisk in 1 egg yolk and bring to a boil, whisking constantly. Boil 1 minute, still whisking.

2 ▲ Remove from the heat. Stir in 2 tablespoons of the butter and the coffee powder. Let cool slightly.

3 ▲ Divide the coffee mixture among 6 wine glasses. Smooth the tops before the mixture sets.

4 ▲ Wipe any dribbles on the insides and outsides of the glasses with a damp paper towel.

5 ▲ For the vanilla layer, combine ½ cup of the sugar and 2 tablespoons of the cornstarch in a heavy saucepan. Gradually whisk in 1⅓ cups of the milk until well blended. Over medium heat, whisk in 1 egg yolk and bring to a boil, whisking. Boil 1 minute.

6 Remove from the heat and stir in 2 tablespoons of the butter and the vanilla. Let cool slightly, then spoon into the glasses on top of the coffee layer. Smooth the tops and wipe the glasses with paper towel.

7 ▲ For the chocolate layer, combine the remaining sugar and cornstarch in a heavy saucepan. Gradually whisk in the remaining milk until well blended. Over moderate heat, whisk in the last egg yolk and bring to a boil, whisking constantly. Boil 1 minute. Off the heat, stir in the remaining butter and the cocoa powder. Let cool slightly, then spoon into the glasses on top of the vanilla layer. Chill until set.

8 ▲ Pipe or spoon whipped cream on top of each pudding before serving.

~ COOK'S TIP ~

For a special occasion, prepare the vanilla layer using a fresh vanilla bean. Choose a plump, supple bean and split it down the center with a sharp knife. Add to the mixture with the milk and discard the bean before spooning into the glasses. The flavor will be more pronounced and the pudding will have pretty brown speckles from the vanilla seeds.

INDEX
~

A

acorn squash: baked acorn
  squash with herbs, 110
  caramel-baked acorn
  squash, 110
apples: apple brown Betty, 41
  apple fritters, 122
  apple maple dumplings, 121
  applesauce cookies, 126
  baked apples, 247
  baked pork loin with red
  cabbage and apples, 106
  pork chops with cider and
  apples, 230
Arizona jalapeño-onion
  quiche, 134
artichoke pasta salad, 180
asparagus: asparagus with
  creamy raspberry
  vinaigrette, 181
  chilled asparagus soup, 11
avocado: avocado dressing,
  204
  guacamole, 156
  lemon chicken with
  guacamole sauce, 190
  Miami chilled avocado
  soup, 50
  Palm Beach papaya and
  avocado salad, 52
  Sante Fe shrimp salad, 136
  turkey and avocado pita
  pizzas, 175

B

bacon: bacon-stuffed potato
  skins, 224
  cheddar and bacon biscuits,
  112
  dandelion salad with hot
  bacon dressing, 94
  tomato-blue cheese soup
  with bacon, 216
  trout and bacon hash, 219
  warm salad of black-eyed
  peas, 53
baked acorn squash with
  herbs, 110
baked apples, 247
baked beans, Boston, 32
baked peaches with raspberry
  sauce, 207
baked pork loin with red
  cabbage and apples, 106

baked scrod, 20
bananas: banana lemon layer
  cake, 83
  chocolate cinnamon cake
  with banana sauce, 162
  Mexican hot fudge
  sundaes, 164
basil: Cajun "popcorn" with
  basil mayonnaise, 57
  roast leg of lamb with
  pesto, 197
beans: bean dip, 161
  black bean burritos, 140
  black bean chili, 141
  Boston baked beans, 32
  huevos rancheros, 132
  pinto bean salad, 137
  spicy bean soup, 131
  three-bean and lentil salad,
  179
beef: beef and eggplant stir-
  fry with ginger, 198
  beef enchiladas, 152
  California taco salad with
  beef, 182
  country meat loaf, 104
  Idaho beef stew, 236
  Indian beef and berry soup,
  92
  lone star steak and potato
  dinner, 154
  Oregon blue cheese
  burgers, 234
  red flannel hash with
  corned beef, 30
  spicy sauerbraten with
  gingersnap gravy, 108
  steak with mushrooms and
  leeks in red wine, 235
  tamale pie, 151
  twin cities meatballs, 103
  Yankee pot roast, 28
beer: pork braised in beer,
  231
beets: Harvard beets, 32
  pickled eggs and beets, 116
  red flannel hash with
  corned beef, 31
beignets: French Quarter
  beignets, 79
bell peppers: chiles rellenos,
  138
  swordfish with bell pepper-
  orange relish, 186
  warm salad of black-eyed
  peas, 53

berries: berry salsa, 200
  Indian beef and berry soup,
  92
  Shaker summer pudding, 40
  see also blackberries;
  blueberries, etc.
biscuits: cheddar and bacon
  biscuits, 112
  cornmeal biscuits, 78
  sausage gravy on biscuits,
  102
  sweet potato biscuits, 37
  Wisconsin cheddar and
  chive biscuits, 112
black beans: black bean
  burritos, 140
  black bean chili, 141
  spicy bean soup, 131
black-eyed peas: warm salad
  of black-eyed peas, 53
black walnut layer cake, 124
blackberries: blackberry
  cobbler, 246
  Indian beef and berry soup,
  92
  Shaker summer pudding, 40
blackened catfish fillets, 71
blackened chicken breasts, 71
blue cheese-chive pennies,
  240
blueberries: blueberry-
  hazelnut cheesecake,
  248
  Maryland peach and
  blueberry pie, 42
Boston baked beans, 32
Boston brown bread, 36
Boston cream pie, 38
bread: Boston brown bread,
  36
  Charleston cheese corn
  bread, 76
  Navajo fry bread, 160
  Shaker summer pudding, 40
  spoonbread, 75
  tomato sandwiches with
  olive mayonnaise, 172
bread and butter pickles,
  116
brethren's cider pie, 44
broccoli: fusilli with turkey,
  tomatoes and broccoli,
  193
brown sugar pie, 120
burritos: black bean burritos,
  140

C

cabbage: baked pork loin
  with red cabbage and
  apples, 106
  coleslaw, 34
Cajun "popcorn" with basil
  mayonnaise, 57
cakes: banana lemon layer
  cake, 83
  black walnut layer cake, 124
  Boston cream pie, 38
  chocolate cinnamon cake
  with banana sauce, 162
  huckleberry coffee cake, 115
  lemon pound cake, 210
  Mississippi mud cake, 82
California taco salad with
  beef, 182
California taco salad with
  chicken, 182
Cape Cod fried clams, 16
caramel: caramel-baked
  acorn squash, 110
  flan, 168
carrots: mashed carrots and
  parsnips, 110
  pot-roasted veal chops with
  carrots, 237
casseroles see stews and
  casseroles
catfish: blackened catfish
  fillets, 71
  fried catfish fillets with
  piquant sauce, 63
cauliflower: cauliflower au
  gratin, 238
celery: stuffed celery sticks,
  96
Charleston cheese corn
  bread, 76
cheddar and bacon biscuits,
  112
cheese: blue cheese-chive
  pennies, 240
  cauliflower au gratin, 238
  Charleston cheese corn
  bread, 76
  cheddar and bacon biscuits,
  112
  chiles rellenos, 138
  dilled smoked salmon
  spread, 240
  fromajardis, 54
  goat cheese salad, 178
  herbed goat cheese dip, 204

huevos rancheros, 132
individual goat cheese
tarts, 174
macaroni and blue cheese,
217
Oregon blue cheese
burgers, 234
stuffed celery sticks, 96
stuffed potato skins, 224
tomato-blue cheese soup
with bacon, 216
Wisconsin cheddar and
chive biscuits, 112
zucchini-cheese casserole,
184
cheesecake: blueberry-
hazelnut cheesecake,
248
cherries: cherry compote, 122
Chesapeake melon and crab
meat salad, 12
Chicago deep-pan pizza, 98
chicken: blackened chicken
breasts, 71
California taco salad with
chicken, 182
chicken Brunswick stew, 26
chicken with white wine,
olives, and garlic, 194
chicken tacos, 146
chicken-mushroom pie, 232
dirty rice, 74
Galveston chicken, 144
lemon chicken with
guacamole sauce, 190
oven "fried" chicken, 70
pan-fried honey chicken
drumsticks, 100
San Francisco chicken
wings, 185
tortilla soup, 130
chili: black bean chili, 141
clam and sausage chili, 227
vegetable chili, 95
chilies: chiles rellenos, 138
pork chops with chili-
nectarine relish, 196
pork chops with sour green
chili salsa, 148
tomato salsa, 156
see also jalapeños
chilled asparagus soup, 11
chives: blue cheese-chive
pennies, 240
Wisconsin cheddar and
chive biscuits, 112

chocolate: Boston cream pie,
38
chocolate cinnamon cake
with banana sauce, 162
chocolate, coconut and
macadamia parfait, 208
chocolate-coffee-vanilla
pudding cups 250
Mississippi mud cake, 82
toffee bars, 126
winter warmer, 242
chorizo: turkey-chorizo tacos,
146
chowders see soups and
chowders
chutney: fresh pineapple-
mint chutney, 201
cider: brethren's cider pie, 44
pork chops with cider and
apples, 230
cioppino, 188
clams: Cape Cod fried clams,
16
clam and sausage chili, 227
New England clam
chowder, 10
spaghetti with clams, 23
coconut: chocolate, coconut
and macadamia parfait,
208
piña colada fruit salad, 210
Southern ambrosia, 84
coffee: chocolate-coffee-
vanilla pudding cups 250
ham with red-eye gravy, 68
Idaho beef stew, 236
Mexican hot fudge
sundaes, 164
Mississippi mud cake, 82
coffee cake: huckleberry
coffee cake, 115
coleslaw, 34
collards and rice, 72
cookies: applesauce cookies,
126
New Mexico Christmas
biscochitos, 165
toffee bars, 126
corn: Charleston cheese corn
bread, 76
chicken Brunswick stew, 26
corn maque choux, 72
corn oysters, 112
Maine broiled lobster
dinner, 24
shrimp and corn bisque, 51

turkey breasts with tomato-
corn salsa, 145
Cornish hens with raisin-
walnut stuffing, 192
corned beef: red flannel hash
with corned beef, 30
cornmeal: Charleston cheese
corn bread, 76
cornmeal biscuits, 78
cornmeal-coated Gulf
shrimp, 143
hush puppies, 76
lamb stew with cornmeal
dumplings, 150
Philadelphia scrapple, 30
spoonbread, 75
tamale pie, 151
country meat loaf, 104
crab: Chesapeake melon and
crab meat salad, 12
crab Bayou, 56
crab Louis, 176
crab soufflé, 25
Maryland crab cakes with
tartar sauce, 18
Old Westbury flounder
with crab, 20
seafood and sausage gumbo,
64
cranberry ice, 46
crawfish: Cajun "popcorn"
with basil mayonnaise,
57
crawfish or shrimp etouffée,
60
cucumber: bread and butter
pickles, 116
custard: flan, 168
Vermont baked maple
custard, 46

D
desert nachos, 132
dill: dilled smoked salmon
spread, 240
dips: avocado dressing, 204
bean dip, 161
guacamole, 156
herbed goat cheese dip,
204
dirty rice, 74
dressings: avocado dressing,
204
dried fruit: Pueblo pastelitos,
166

E
easy hazelnut fudge, 242
easy peanut butter fudge, 242
eggplant: beef and eggplant
stir-fry with ginger, 198
eggplant ratatouille, 202
shrimp-stuffed eggplant, 58
eggs: eggs Benedict, 17
huevos rancheros, 132
pickled eggs and beets, 116
San Antonio tortilla, 135
stuffed deviled eggs, 96
enchilada sauce, 158
enchiladas: beef enchiladas,
152

F
fajitas: pork fajitas, 149
fish: cioppino, 188
Seattle fish fritters, 220
see also catfish; flounder etc.
flan, 168
flounder: Old Westbury
flounder with crab, 20
fresh pineapple-mint
chutney, 201
French Quarter beignets, 79
fried catfish fillets with
piquant sauce, 63
fried tomatoes with ham, 34
fromajardis, 54
fruit: berry salsa, 200
piña colada fruit salad, 210
Shaker summer pudding, 40
see also apples; bananas etc.
fudge: easy hazelnut fudge,
242
easy peanut butter fudge,
242
Mexican hot fudge
sundaes, 164
fusilli with turkey, tomatoes
and broccoli, 193

G
Galveston chicken, 144
garlicky sautéed zucchini, 202
gazpacho, 173
Georgia peanut butter pie, 80
ginger: beef and eggplant stir-
fry with ginger, 198
spicy sauerbraten with
gingersnap gravy, 108

goat cheese: goat cheese salad, 178

   herbed goat cheese dip, 204

   individual goat cheese tarts, 174

grapefruit: pink grapefruit sherbet, 86

guacamole: guacamole, 156

   lemon chicken with guacamole sauce, 190

gumbo: seafood and sausage gumbo, 64

H

ham: fried tomatoes with ham, 34

   ham with red-eye gravy, 68

   pirozhki with ham filling, 99

Harvard beets, 32

hazelnuts: blueberry-hazelnut cheesecake, 248

   easy hazelnut fudge, 242

herbed goat cheese dip, 204

herbs: salmon with sizzling herbs, 229

   see also basil; chives *etc.*

horseradish: pan-fried trout with horseradish sauce, 228

huckleberries: huckleberry coffee cake, 115

   Indian beef and berry soup, 92

huevos rancheros, 132

hush puppies, 76

I

ice cream: chocolate, coconut, and macadamia ·parfait, 208

   Mexican hot fudge sundaes, 164

Idaho beef stew, 236

Indian beef and berry soup, 92

individual goat cheese tarts, 174

J

jalapeños: Arizona jalapeño-onion quiche, 134

   berry salsa, 200

   desert nachos, 132

K

kabobs: Long Island scallop and mussel kabobs, 13

   shrimp kabobs with plum sauce, 189

key lime sherbet, 87

kiwi fruit: piña colada fruit salad, 210

L

lamb: lamb stew with cornmeal dumplings, 150

   roast leg of lamb with pesto, 197

leeks: chilled asparagus soup, 11

   steak with mushrooms and leeks in red wine, 235

lemons: banana lemon layer cake, 83

   lemon chicken with guacamole sauce, 190

   lemon pound cake, 210

lentils: smoked turkey and lentil soup, 215

   three-bean and lentil salad, 179

limes: key lime sherbet, 87

lobster: lobster soufflé, 25

   Maine broiled lobster dinner, 24

lone star steak and potato dinner, 154

Long Island scallop and mussel kabobs, 13

M

macadamia nuts: chocolate, coconut and macadamia parfait, 208

macaroni and blue cheese, 217

maple syrup: apple maple dumplings, 121

   brethren's cider pie, 44

   Vermont baked maple custard, 46

Maryland crab cakes with tartar sauce, 18

Maryland peach and blueberry pie, 42

mashed carrots and parsnips, 110

mayonnaise: Cajun "popcorn" with basil mayonnaise, 57

   tomato sandwiches with olive mayonnaise, 172

meat *see* bacon; beef *etc.*

meat loaf: country meat loaf, 104

   turkey meat loaf, 194

melon: Chesapeake melon and crab meat salad, 12

Mexican hot fudge sundaes, 164

Miami chilled avocado soup, 50

Milwaukee onion shortcake, 114

mint: fresh pineapple-mint chutney, 201

Mississippi mud cake, 82

mushrooms: chicken-mushroom pie, 232

   steak with mushrooms and leeks in red wine, 235

mussels: cioppino, 188

   Long Island scallop and mussel kabobs, 13

   Penn Cove steamed mussels, 223

N

nachos: desert nachos, 132

Navajo fry bread, 160

nectarines: pork chops with chili-nectarine relish, 196

New England clam chowder, 10

New Mexico Christmas biscochitos, 165

Northwestern brown betty, 244

nuts *see* hazelnuts; macadamia nuts *etc.*

O

oatmeal pan-fried trout, 100

Old Westbury flounder with crab, 20

olives: chicken with white wine, olives, and garlic, 194

   tomato sandwiches with olive mayonnaise, 172

onions: Arizona jalapeño-onion quiche, 134

   bread and butter pickles, 116

   Milwaukee onion shortcake, 114

   onion rivel soup, 90

oranges: orange sherbet, 86

   Southern ambrosia, 84

   tangerine-soy marinated salmon, 187

Oregon blue cheese burgers, 234

oven "fried" chicken, 70

oysters: oyster stew, 14

   oysters Rockefeller, 14

   scalloped oysters, 222

P

Palm Beach papaya and avocado salad, 52

pan-fried honey chicken drumsticks, 100

pan-fried trout with horseradish sauce, 228

papaya: Palm Beach papaya and avocado salad, 52

parsnips: mashed carrots and parsnips, 110

pasta: artichoke pasta salad, 180

   fusilli with turkey, tomatoes and broccoli, 193

   macaroni and blue cheese, 217

   pasta with scallops, 226

   pasta with zucchini sauce, 202

   smoked trout pasta salad, 218

peaches: baked peaches with raspberry sauce, 207

   Maryland peach and blueberry pie, 42

peanut butter: easy peanut butter fudge, 242

   Georgia peanut butter pie, 80

pears: Northwestern brown betty, 244

   zinfandel poached pears, 206

pecans: pecan pralines, 84

   pecan-stuffed pork chops, 68

Penn Cove steamed mussels, 223

Pennsylvania Dutch fried tomatoes, 34
pesto: roast leg of lamb with pesto, 197
Philadelphia scrapple, 30
pickles: bread and butter pickles, 116
  pickled eggs and beets, 116
pies: brethren's cider pie, 44
  brown sugar pie, 120
  chicken-mushroom pie, 232
  Georgia peanut butter pie, 80
  Maryland peach and blueberry pie, 42
  rhubarb pie, 118
piña colada fruit salad, 210
pineapple: fresh pineapple-mint chutney, 201
  piña colada fruit salad, 210
  Southern ambrosia, 84
pink grapefruit sherbet, 86
pinto bean salad, 137
pirozhki with ham filling, 99
pizza: Chicago deep-pan pizza, 98
  turkey and avocado pita pizzas, 175
plums: shrimp kabobs with plum sauce, 189
poolside tuna salad, 176
pork: baked pork loin with red cabbage and apples, 106
  country meat loaf, 104
  dirty rice, 74
  pecan-stuffed pork chops, 68
  Philadelphia scrapple, 30
  pork braised in beer, 231
  pork chops with chili-nectarine relish, 196
  pork chops with cider and apples, 230
  pork chops with sour green chili salsa, 148
  pork fajitas, 149
  pork jambalaya, 67
  spareribs with sauerkraut, 105
  spicy New Mexico pork stew, 146
  twin cities meatballs, 103
pot roast: pot-roasted veal chops with carrots, 237
  yankee pot roast, 28
potatoes: bacon-stuffed potato skins, 224

lone star steak and potato dinner, 154
  San Antonio tortilla, 135
  stuffed potato skins, 224
pralines: pecan pralines, 84
puddings: chocolate-coffee-vanilla pudding cups, 250
  Shaker summer pudding, 40
  Southwestern rice pudding, 169
pueblo pastelitos, 166
pumpkin: spiced pumpkin soup, 92

Q

quiche: Arizona jalapeño-onion quiche, 134

R

rabbit: smothered rabbit, 66
raspberries: asparagus with creamy raspberry vinaigrette, 181
  baked peaches with raspberry sauce, 207
red cabbage: baked pork loin with red cabbage and apples, 106
red flannel hash with corned beef, 30
red snapper with cilantro salsa, 142
relish: pork chops with chili-nectarine relish, 196
  swordfish with bell pepper-orange relish, 186
rhubarb: rhubarb pie, 118
rice: collards and rice, 72
  dirty rice, 74
  Southwestern rice pudding, 169
  tomato rice, 158
  wild rice pilaf, 239
roast leg of lamb with pesto, 197

S

salad: artichoke pasta salad, 180
  California taco salad with beef, 182
  California taco salad with chicken, 182

Chesapeake melon and crab meat salad, 12
  goat cheese salad, 178
  Palm Beach papaya and avocado salad, 52
  pinto bean salad, 137
  poolside tuna salad, 176
  Santa Fe shrimp salad, 136
  smoked trout pasta salad, 218
  three-bean and lentil salad, 179
  warm salad of black-eyed peas, 53
salmon: dilled smoked salmon spread, 240
  salmon chowder, 214
  salmon with sizzling herbs, 229
  Seattle fish fritters, 220
  Seattle salmon fritters, 220
  tangerine-soy marinated salmon, 187
salsa: berry salsa, 200
  pork chops with sour green chili salsa, 148
  red snapper with cilantro salsa, 142
  tomato salsa, 156
  turkey breasts with tomato-corn salsa, 145
San Antonio tortilla, 135
sandwiches: Oregon blue cheese burgers, 234
  tomato sandwiches with olive mayonnaise, 172
San Francisco chicken wings, 185
Santa Fe shrimp salad, 136
sauerkraut: spareribs with sauerkraut, 105
sausage: clam and sausage chili, 227
  sausage gravy on biscuits, 102
  seafood and sausage gumbo, 64
scalloped oysters, 222
scallops: Long Island scallop and mussel kabobs, 13
  pasta with scallops, 226
  scallops thermidor, 22
scrod: baked scrod, 20
seafood: seafood and sausage gumbo, 64
  see also crab; crawfish etc.

Seattle fish fritters, 220
Seattle salmon fritters, 220
Shaker summer pudding, 40
sherbet: cranberry ice, 46
  key lime sherbet, 87
  orange sherbet, 86
  pink grapefruit sherbet, 86
shrimp: Cajun "popcorn" with basil mayonnaise, 57
  cornmeal-coated Gulf shrimp, 143
  crawfish or shrimp etouffée, 60
  Santa Fe shrimp salad, 136
  seafood and sausage gumbo, 64
  Seattle fish fritters, 220
  shrimp and corn bisque, 51
  shrimp Creole, 62
  shrimp kabobs with plum sauce, 189
  shrimp soufflé, 25
  shrimp-stuffed eggplant, 58
smoked salmon: dilled smoked salmon spread, 240
smoked trout pasta salad, 218
smoked turkey and lentil soup, 215
smothered rabbit, 66
soups and chowders: chilled asparagus soup, 11
  cioppino, 188
  gazpacho, 173
  Miami chilled avocado soup, 50
  New England clam chowder, 10
  onion rivel soup, 90
  oyster stew, 14
  salmon chowder, 214
  shrimp and corn bisque, 51
  smoked turkey and lentil soup, 215
  spiced pumpkin soup, 92
  spicy bean soup, 131
  split pea soup, 91
  tomato-blue cheese soup with bacon, 216
  tortilla soup, 130
Southern ambrosia, 84
spaghetti with clams, 23
spareribs with sauerkraut, 105
spicy bean soup, 131
spicy New Mexico pork stew, 146

spicy sauerbraten with gingersnap gravy, 108
split peas: split pea soup, 91
spoonbread, 75
squid: cioppino, 188
steak: lone star steak and potato dinner, 154
steak with mushrooms and leeks in red wine, 235
stews and casseroles: chicken Brunswick stew, 26
Idaho beef stew, 236
lamb stew with cornmeal dumplings, 150
oyster stew, 14
spicy New Mexico pork stew, 146
zucchini-cheese casserole, 184
strawberries: berry salsa, 200
piña colada fruit salad, 210
rhubarb-strawberry crisp, 245
stuffed celery sticks, 96
stuffed deviled eggs, 96
stuffed potato skins, 224
sweet potato biscuits, 37
swordfish with bell pepper-orange relish, 186

T

tacos: chicken tacos, 146
turkey-chorizo tacos, 146
tamale pie, 151

tangerine-soy marinated salmon, 187
tarts, individual goat cheese, 174
three-bean and lentil salad, 179
toffee bars, 126
tomatoes: enchilada sauce, 158
fried tomatoes with ham, 34
fusilli with turkey, tomatoes and broccoli, 193
Pennsylvania Dutch fried tomatoes, 34
stuffed cherry tomatoes, 96
tomato-blue cheese soup with bacon, 216
tomato rice, 158
tomato salsa, 156
tomato sandwiches with olive mayonnaise, 172
turkey breasts with tomato-corn salsa, 145
tortilla chips: bean dip, 161
California taco salad with beef, 182
California taco salad with chicken, 182
desert nachos, 132
tortillas: beef enchiladas, 152
pork fajitas, 149
San Antonio tortilla, 135
tortilla soup, 130
trout: oatmeal pan-fried trout, 100

pan-fried trout with horseradish sauce, 228
smoked trout pasta salad, 218
trout and bacon hash, 219
tuna: poolside tuna salad, 176
turkey: fusilli with turkey, tomatoes and broccoli, 193
smoked turkey and lentil soup, 215
turkey and avocado pita pizzas, 175
turkey breasts with tomato-corn salsa, 145
turkey-chorizo tacos, 146
turkey meat loaf, 194
twin cities meatballs, 103

V

vanilla: chocolate-coffee-vanilla pudding cups 250
veal: country meat loaf, 104
pot-roasted veal chops with carrots, 237
twin cities meatballs, 103
vegetables: gazpacho, 173
tortilla soup, 130
vegetable chili, 95
see also acorn squash; asparagus etc.
venison: spicy sauerbraten with gingersnap gravy, 108

W

walnuts: black walnut layer cake, 124
Cornish hens with raisin-walnut stuffing, 192
warm salad of black-eyed peas, 53
wild rice pilaf, 239
wine: chicken with white wine, olives, and garlic, 194
steak with mushrooms and leeks in red wine, 235
zinfandel poached pears, 206
winter warmer (hot white chocolate), 242
Wisconsin cheddar and chiv biscuits, 112

Y

yankee pot roast, 28

Z

zinfandel poached pears, 206
zucchini: garlicky sautéed zucchini, 202
pasta with zucchini sauce, 202
zucchini-cheese casserole, 184